)

TRANSLATIONS FROM GREEK AND ROMAN AUTHORS

Series Editor: GRAHAM TINGAY

LIVY
Stories of Rome

Translated by ROGER NICHOLS

CAMBRIDGE UNIVERSITY PRESS

Cambridge
London   New York   New Rochelle
Melbourne   Sydney

Published by the Press Syndicate of the University of Cambridge
The Pitt Building, Trumpington Street, Cambridge CB2 1RP
32 East 57th Street, New York, NY 10022, USA
296 Beaconsfield Parade, Middle Park, Melbourne 3206, Australia

First published 1982

Printed in Great Britain by Redwood Burn Limited, Trowbridge, Wiltshire

Library of Congress catalogue card number: 81-10227

British Library Cataloguing in Publication Data
Livy
[Ab urbe condita. *English*. *Selections*]. Stories of Rome.
1. Rome – History
I. Title II. Nichols, Roger III. Stories of Rome
937   DG27
ISBN 0 521 22816 6

Maps by Reg Piggott

The bronze figure of the legendary
she-wolf (see p. 8) on the front
cover is Etruscan. The illustration
is reproduced by courtesy of
Mansell-Alinan

Contents

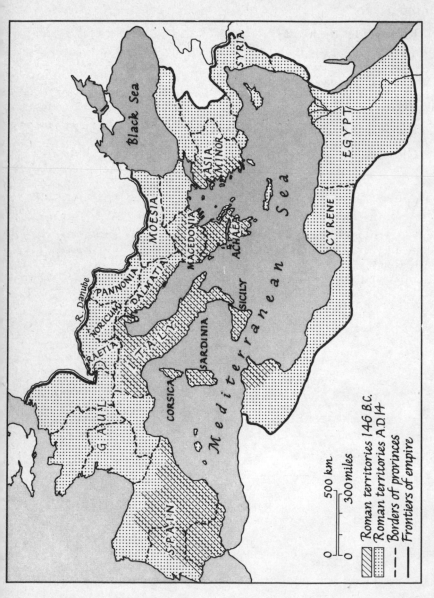

Roman territories in 146 B.C. and A.D. 14

Introduction

Two thousand years ago Titus Livius, whom we know as Livy, was writing the history of Rome and its empire. Rome itself was then the greatest city in the world; the empire, though it was to become still larger and richer in the next five hundred years, even in Livy's time embraced much of Europe, North Africa and the Middle East (see map, p. iv). It had all started some eight hundred years earlier, when there had been a group of tiny villages overlooking the river Tiber, the settlement of a few shepherds and farmers. According to Roman tradition, in 753 B.C. a city had been founded by Romulus, the first of seven kings: it is likely that this 'foundation' represents the union of these villages, for clearly, if they joined together, they would be better able to defend themselves and take advantage of the commercial opportunity of their site, right next to the major ford of the river.

Whatever the facts may be, we know that throughout the period of the kings (753-510 B.C.) Rome was largely under the influence of the Etruscans. These were a powerful people occupying the land to the north of Rome; they lived in handsome, well-fortified cities, and were skilled in a wide range of industries – textiles, mining and metal-work, for example – and traded extensively with Greece and the Middle East, the area from which they had probably migrated to Italy. Of the seven kings of Rome – Romulus, Numa Pompilius, Tullus Hostilius, Ancus Martius, Tarquinius Priscus, Servius Tullius and Tarquinius Superbus – both the Tarquins were Etruscan, and Rome must have fallen completely under Etruscan sway. It was during the reign of the last three kings that the low-lying swampland between the hills was drained and transformed into a *forum*,* or market-place, and Rome grew from a mere settlement into a proper city, with defensive ramparts, public buildings and temples.

When Etruscan power declined – and we simply do not know why it did – Rome expelled the last Etruscan king and became an independent republic, governed by a council of the most influential citizens, called the Senate. Each year the senators elected from their number two senior magistrates, known first as praetors, but later as consuls.* Their function was to summon the Senate, preside over its discussions, carry out its instructions and, most important of all, to command the armies of Rome in war. The new republic soon began to control most of the Tiber valley, from the mountains to the sea, as well as the land to the south, so that Rome became much the most

1

powerful city in the plain of Latium (see map, p. 6). But the other Latin cities were not prepared to accept Roman domination; they joined together to fight for their independence, and Rome had for the moment to give up any hope of supremacy. For much of the next hundred years Rome was merely an equal partner in a Latin alliance, fully occupied in defending the fertile plain of Latium from the raids of fierce mountain tribes – the Volsci, Aequi and Sabini.

But Rome was not destined for mediocrity: by 390 B.C. she had become the most powerful member of the Latin alliance. Yet her hopes of supremacy were dashed once again, for a marauding tribe of Gauls defeated her army, destroyed most of the city, and only departed when 1,000 lb (450 kg) of gold were handed over. Despite this massive setback, within fifty years Rome had risen from the ashes to overcome the other Latin cities and become supreme in Latium. Wars against the Samnites in central Italy, and then against the Greek states in the south followed; by 278 B.C., through conquest and shrewd alliances, and by granting various degrees of independence to her defeated enemies, Rome emerged as the undisputed leader of all Italy south of the river Rubicon.

While Rome had been struggling for supremacy in Italy there had been an equally bitter feud on home ground, between the patricians* and plebeians – the land-owning aristocracy against the rest of the populace. Soon after the republic was formed, the plebeians resorted to strike action, refusing to fight in the army, until they were allowed to elect their own officers – *tribuni plebis,* tribunes of the people* – to protect them against arrogant magistrates. Gradually the plebeians acquired wider legal rights and a larger control over their own lives, till in 287 B.C. resolutions of the Assembly of the People, called *plebiscita,* acquired the force of law binding on the whole populace. But before the plebeians could gain much advantage from their new powers Rome was drawn, almost unwillingly, into a long conflict with Carthage, the great trading power of the western Mediterranean, which did not end till the defeat of Hannibal in 202 B.C. Sicily, Corsica, Sardinia and Spain were the prize that fell to Rome, to form her overseas empire; Greece, modern Tunisia (the Roman province of Africa) and Asia Minor (north-western Turkey) were added by 133 B.C. Year by year more lands bordering or near the Mediterranean submitted to Rome. When Livy died in A.D. 17 the empire was almost complete, defended and defined by great natural frontiers – seas, rivers and deserts (see map, p. iv).

Overseas conquest, however, had not brought internal peace or happiness. The power and wealth of the new empire fell into the hands of the rich senators, while all the blood, sweat and toil came from the plebeians. Appian, another historian of Rome in the second century A.D. wrote this summary:

The rich took possession of most of the state land, and grew confident, as time passed, that no one would take this land away from them. Then they absorbed any adjoining strips of land, and the small-holdings of their poor neighbours, buying some of them and taking others by force. In this way they began to cultivate vast tracts instead of single estates. They used slaves as agricultural labourers and herdsmen, instead of free men who were likely to be taken from the land and conscripted into the army. In this way some powerful men became extremely rich, and their slaves increased in number because they were exempt from serving in the army. But the poor dwindled in number under the burdens of poverty, taxation and military service. And if they did escape these hardships they passed their time in idleness because the rich owned the land, and used slaves, not free men, to work it.

But in 133 B.C. Tiberius Gracchus, a tribune of the people, challenged the rich landowners by resorting to the powers of the Assembly of the People, dormant since 287 B.C., to pass a law re-allocating some of the state land to Rome's unemployed plebeians. Ten years later his brother Gaius went further and transferred some political power to the next most powerful class outside the Senate, the *equites* or knights. Since members of the Senatorial Order were forbidden by law from taking part in any business activity that was not connected with their possession of land, the equites controlled the trading and finance companies of the growing empire.

For most of the next century there was a bitter struggle for power between the magistrates, Senate, equites and Plebeians. Marius, consul in 107 and from 104 to 100 B.C., and a great favourite of the people, had to wear down Rome's enemies in Africa and then destroy huge tribes of Gauls and Teutons invading Italy over the Alps: to do so he created a new, efficient, almost professional army. Unhappily the Senate never learnt how to control the army or its commanders. A grim civil war raged between Rome and some of her Italian allies until citizenship was granted to them all. Sulla, who was a strong supporter of the Senate, deprived of an overseas command by Marius and a conniving tribune, marched his legions into Rome, killed the tribune and drove Marius into ignominious flight. He then left for his Middle East command. Marius in turn raised legions, seized Rome and butchered his political opponents wholesale till he died suddenly (perhaps of a heart attack) in 86 B.C. Sulla fought his way back into Italy four years later, set himself up as Dictator,* and hounded *his* political opponents to death, till he succumbed to disease in 78 B.C. The consul of that year, Lepidus, marched his troops on Rome in a vain attempt to overthrow the constitution, and died in exile. Seventy thousand escaped slaves terrorised Italy for two years till slaughtered by Crassus and Pompey, who both immediately demanded, and got, the consulship.

Against all this the Senate was virtually powerless – it was still a town council rather than the administrative power centre of a vast empire. When it did try to assert its authority, it managed to snub Pompey, Crassus and Caesar all in one year. Consequently they formed an alliance, known as the First Triumvirate, and backed by troops who saw no point in loyalty to a miserly Senate, dominated the state. Caesar set out to conquer Gaul (which took him ten years), Crassus was killed in Parthia during a campaign intended primarily to increase his already enormous personal wealth, and Pompey was slowly weaned from his alliance with Caesar by the conservative aristocracy. Civil war broke out again in 49 B.C. Though Pompey was soon defeated and killed, Caesar had to fight a series of merciless battles against his supporters till final victory in 45 B.C. Within a year Caesar had been declared Dictator for life, and was swiftly assassinated. There followed yet more civil strife, and a Second Triumvirate, between Mark Antony, Octavian (Caesar's eighteen-year-old heir) and another Lepidus, a comparative nonentity. The empire was divided: broadly speaking, Octavian was assigned Italy and the Western provinces, and Antony the East. A final struggle between the two was inevitable. A naval battle off the coast of Greece in 31 B.C., the suicide of Antony and Cleopatra in Egypt in the following year, and at long last the dreary tale of bloodshed and war was over.

Octavian became sole emperor, with a new name – Augustus – and slowly the world began to put aside its fears and rebuild hope and confidence in the future.

It was in this climate of lingering suspicion and gathering hopes that Livy wrote. In the introduction to his massive work – it contained 142 books, of which 35 survive – he explained his purpose. He wanted to describe the men and morals that had brought Rome her early greatness and empire, and then to recount the decline of morals and the weaknesses that had led to the appalling troubles of the last hundred years. Livy felt that there was no hope for the future unless moral standards improved. For men cannot escape their fate – which exists apart from the gods as a general scheme of things controlling the world at large and the men in it, and in the end ensures that justice is done. His intention was both to entertain and to instruct, and the lesson that his reader should learn must be plain. He does not say whether he believes in the legends of Rome's early history, and clearly some *are* pure fancy; but he does not care. If they are not true, they are at least like the truth, and they ought to be true. They illustrate the old Roman character that Livy so much admired, and that is what he considered important. He appears to have relied on the works of earlier historians, without carefully checking facts or examining closely whatever original records had survived. He knew little about military matters, not much more about politics, and nothing of economics. Meticulous accuracy was unimportant for his readers. But his enthusiasm was complete and infectious, and his gift for dramatic narrative or vivid character sketches was outstanding, and won him immediate acceptance and praise. The first of the many English translations appeared in the reign of Elizabeth I: they have, as you see, never stopped.

Note: words marked with an asterisk are explained in the Glossary, p. 91.

Index of passages translated

Some of the passages listed below have not been translated in their entirety, but have been abridged or cut.

Rome and her neighbours in the fifth century B.C.

1 Rome under the kings

You have probably heard some of the stories about the Trojan War – and how after ten years Troy was captured and the Greeks went home. The history of Rome really goes back to the adventures of the defeated Trojans. As their city was completely gutted, they had to find a new home. Their leader, Aeneas, eventually brought them to the west coast of Italy. He married Lavinia, the daughter of a local king called Latinus, and gave the name Lavinium to the first town he founded. Aeneas' son, Ascanius, left Lavinium and built a settlement of his own in the Alban hills. Because it was a long, straggly town on a ridge, he called it Alba Longa (see map, p. 6).

After Ascanius, Alba Longa had a number of kings. The thirteenth was called Proca, and it is with him that the story of Rome really begins.

THE CITY OF ROMULUS

Proca had two sons, Numitor and Amulius. He left the kingdom to Numitor, as he was the elder of the two brothers. But Amulius had more respect for force than for his father's ideas, or for his brother's seniority. He drove Numitor out and took over the kingdom. Not satisfied with that, he went on to assassinate Numitor's sons and made his daughter, Rea Silvia, a Vestal Virgin.* On the surface this seemed to be a mark of respect, but in fact it meant she had to stay a virgin for the rest of her life. She was meant to be the last of Numitor's family.

But, as I see it, the Fates were already planning the foundation of our great city which has become the centre of an empire second only to that of the gods. Rea Silvia was raped and produced twins. She claimed that Mars was the father. Perhaps she really believed it, or perhaps she just thought that if someone had to take the blame, a god would make the whole thing more respectable. In any case both mortals and immortals proved powerless to protect her and her baby sons from Amulius' savage fury. Silvia herself was tied up and thrown into prison. Amulius ordered her boys, Romulus and Remus, to be dumped in the river.

However, some god was on their side. The Tiber was in flood – it had burst its banks and water lay all round it in stagnant pools. As a result the king's slaves couldn't reach the Tiber itself. But even though the floodwater was sluggish they still thought there was a good chance that the babies would drown. So they carried out their orders, more or less, and left the children in the nearest pool of water – in fact where the Ruminal fig-tree is now (apparently it was once called 'the fig-tree of Romulus').

In those days the whole place was uninhabited for miles around. The story goes that the floodwater receded from where the boys were, leaving them high and dry. A she-wolf was on her way down from the hills to have a drink in the river, when she heard them yelling. She went to look, and offered them her teats to suck. Indeed the animal was so motherly that she started licking them, and this was the scene that greeted the king's shepherd. Faustulus (that's the name he's usually given) then took the children back to his hut and handed them over to his wife Larentia to look after. (Some people think Larentia was a prostitute and so the shepherds called her 'the she-wolf'. It could be an explanation of this fable.)

So Romulus and Remus grew up and from their early teens they threw themselves into their work, helping on the farm, minding the flock, hunting in the forest. They grew tough, in mind and body. From hunting wild animals they moved on to ambushing robbers and relieving them of their ill-gotten gains. These would be shared out between their friends, an ever-growing gang of young shepherds, who revelled in hard work as well as less serious pursuits.

People say that even in those distant days the Palatine hill was the setting for the festival of the Lupercalia. In honour of the god Pan, young men ran about naked and generally misbehaved themselves. This festival took place at the same season each year, so the robbers seized the opportunity to avenge themselves for what they had lost. They launched an attack. Romulus fought them off but they managed to get Remus. Then they dragged him before King Amulius and brought charges against him: first, that he and his brother were always trespassing on land belonging to ex-king Numitor, and second, that they were the leaders of a gang of youths who were stealing his cattle. So Amulius handed the young man over to Numitor to be dealt with.

Now, right from the start, Faustulus had suspected that the two boys he was bringing up were the royal twins. After all, he knew about the king's instructions and also that he had found two children at exactly the same moment. But he had decided not to say anything until the time seemed ripe, or until he was forced to. And now he was forced to. Trembling with fear, he told Romulus the whole story.

Numitor too had been thinking about his grandchildren. He was told that the young man in his custody was one of twins. He considered the young man's age and his distinctly un-slavelike character. After making some further enquiries he was on the point of acknowledging Remus as his grandson. The net began to close in round Amulius. Romulus did not have the forces for a direct attack; instead he told small groups of shepherds to make their way to the palace independently, and the assault began. They were joined by another group coming from Numitor's house with Remus in charge. And so Amulius was slaughtered.

While the first blows were being struck Numitor raised a false alarm. 'It's an enemy attack', he shouted, 'they're inside the walls and storming the palace.' He summoned the young men of Alba Longa to form a garrison at the central fortress of the town and defend it by force. Then he saw the twins coming towards him. From their triumphant expressions he knew that the deed was done. At once he called all the townspeople together and spoke to them: of the crimes his brother had committed against him, of his grandsons' birth, their upbringing and how their true identity had been discovered – finally he told them that the tyrant had been murdered and that he, Numitor, was the man responsible. As he was speaking the two young men marched into the meeting at the head of their private army. 'Numitor for king!' they shouted. 'Numitor for king!' came the reply from the whole crowd. So the old man was restored to his throne.

With Alba Longa now in Numitor's safe keeping, Romulus and Remus set their hearts on founding a new city, in the area where they had been abandoned and then brought up. In Alba Longa itself and round about there was a large surplus population. And with the shepherds as well, it seemed likely that one day both Alba and Lavinium would be dwarfed by this new settlement. But the plan was soon interrupted. Like Amulius and Numitor, Romulus and Remus were both ruthlessly determined to be king. So, from a peaceful beginning sprang rivalry and bitterness. As they were twins, it was impossible to decide simply on the basis of their ages. Instead the decision was handed over to the gods who protected the place; by the flight of birds they could decide which

9

of the brothers was to give his name to the new city and rule over it once it was built. To inspect the birds' movements Romulus took up his station on the Palatine hill and Remus on the Aventine.

Remus, they say, was the first to see a sign: six vultures. This sighting had just been announced when a flock of twelve vultures displayed themselves to Romulus. Each of the brothers was then hailed as king by his supporters, shouting 'He saw them first!' and 'He saw twice as many!' The two groups were soon at blows and a pitched battle followed. In this fracas Remus was killed. A more popular version of the story says that Remus jumped over the foundations of the walls on purpose to annoy his brother. Romulus was indeed furious. He shouted at Remus, 'This is how I deal with invaders!' and killed him on the spot. Romulus was now in sole command, and when the city was built it was named after him: Rome.

> The date usually given for the founding of Rome is 753 B.C. Romulus allowed anybody who wanted to to come and live in the city. So it soon filled up with a lot of the down-and-outs and criminals who couldn't find a home anywhere else. As we shall see, this produced problems.

THE SABINE WOMEN

Rome was now strong enough to stand up to any of the nearby tribes. But it looked as though this strength would not continue for more than one generation. The population seemed bound to fall because there were so few women in the city, and so far there had been no marriages between Romans and outsiders. But now the senators suggested that Romulus should send representatives round the towns in the area. He wanted to make alliances with them and persuade them to let their women marry men from Rome.

Everywhere the representatives got a cool reception. Partly it was contempt. But partly it was fear of what this powerful and growing city might one day do, both to themselves and to their descendants. Often the representatives were turned away with taunts such as 'Have you opened your gates to female criminals as well? You could make plenty of suitable matches then!' This sort of remark did not go down well with the young men of Rome. Clearly violence was in the air.

Romulus made up his mind: if there had to be violence, then *he* would choose where and when. So he pretended not to mind these insults. Instead he began to organise Games* in honour of Neptune,* the god of horses. He made it clear that he wanted all the neighbouring towns to know, and the Romans did all they could to make the festival attractive and to spread publicity for it.

A huge crowd turned up. For one thing, they were curious to see what this new town was like. Most of them were from nearby, including the whole population of Sabinum, with their wives and children. The Romans invited them to stay in their homes. Then the visitors went on a tour of the city, looking at the general layout, the fortifications and the large number of private houses. They were amazed at how much had been done in such a short time. Then it was time for the Games. Soon everyone's attention was riveted. This was the moment chosen for the raid. At a given signal, the young Romans dashed into the crowd and grabbed hold of the Sabine girls. Mostly they took the ones who happened to be nearest. Some of the prettier ones, though, had been earmarked as senators' property; they were taken away by specially recruited gangs.

The festival broke up in a panic. The girls' parents rushed off in a terrible state, complaining that the laws of hospitality had been broken. They also prayed to Neptune, to whose festival they had come in good faith, only to be cheated. The girls themselves were just as frantic about what was going to become of them. They were furious too. But Romulus went round and had a word with each of them:

'Really it's your fathers who are to blame. They were too proud to let us marry you. But, now you *are* married, you'll share all our benefits and privileges. What's more, you'll share the greatest blessing of the human race – children. Just calm down! Accept what's happened with a good grace! Rage can often turn to love. And your husbands, I know, will treat you well. They will be trying not only to do their duty as husbands but to make up for the parents and the homes you have left behind you.'

Their new husbands set about flattering them, too, saying 'I only did it because I fell so passionately in love with you' – the sort of thing women find so hard to resist.

Not surprisingly, the outraged visitors decided to fight back. Unfortunately for them, the various tribes could not agree on a plan and Rome was able to pick them off one by one. But the Sabines bided their time.

11

There was nothing wild or hot-headed about the Sabines' campaign. They gave no warning of what they intended to do. Their careful planning included even a measure of treachery. The Roman stronghold was commanded by Spurius Tarpeius. He had a young daughter and one day she went outside the walls to fetch water for a sacrifice. The Sabine king bribed her with gold to let his soldiers into the stronghold. When they did get in, they crushed her to death with their shields. Maybe this was to make it look as if they had captured the stronghold by their own efforts. Or maybe it was their way of saying: 'Never trust a traitor.' Apparently the Sabines used to wear heavy gold bracelets on their left arms and large jewelled rings on their left hands. According to one version of the story, she agreed to betray the city 'in return for what the men are wearing on their left arms'. But instead of gold bracelets, she got shields.

A battle followed and the Romans were getting the worst of it.

The Sabines, led by Mettius Curtius, came rushing down the slope from the stronghold. He drove the Romans headlong, over what is now the forum, and almost up to the Palatine gate.

'We've got them!' he shouted. 'They may be good at cheating, but they can't fight. They've learnt one thing, though. Girl-snatching is a very different business from dealing with men like us.'

In the middle of these brave words, Romulus launched an attack with a small group of his toughest soldiers. At that moment Mettius was on horseback. This made it harder for him to stand his ground. He galloped off, hotly pursued by the Romans. Elsewhere on the battlefield, Romulus' brave example was having its effect. The Sabines were retreating fast. Meanwhile the noise of Romulus' men had scared Mettius' horse. It bolted into a swamp. The Sabines even stopped fighting in order to help their general and, after a lot of shouting and waving of arms, he managed to get out. Then the battle started again in earnest, on the level ground between the two hills. Now the Romans began to win.

At this moment, the Sabine women, without whom there would not have been a battle at all, pushed their way between the two armies, their hair flying and their clothes torn.

'Enough! Stop!' they cried. 'It is a sin for fathers to fight husbands. Think of the disgrace you're bringing to your children – and grandchildren. If you're ashamed of your relationship, of

12

our marriages, why not be furious with us? This family vendetta is all our fault. We would rather die ourselves than be widows or orphans.' Their words had the desired effect. Common soldiers and generals alike were suddenly silent. Then the leaders stepped forward to arrange a truce. So peace was made, and the two communities were united under a single government. Rome was to be the capital.

> Rome went on growing quickly. Romulus was followed as king by Numa Pompilius, and he in turn by Tullus Hostilius. The family name Hostilius suited him. By now, in about 670 B.C., seventy years after Rome had been founded, many of her neighbours were jealous of her, and frightened. Among them was Alba Longa. Cattle raiding led to war. The two armies faced each other, but the Alban leader suggested a way to avoid large-scale bloodshed.

TRIPLE COMBAT: c.670 B.C.

As it so happened, in each army there were three brothers who were triplets. Both sets were also much the same age and build. The two families concerned were the Horatii and the Curiatii, and this is altogether one of the most inspiring of these old stories. (There does seem to be some doubt as to which was on which side, but I will follow the usual version and call the Romans the Horatii.) The two leaders, Tullus and Mettius, put a proposal to the triplets: 'Fight each other for your country, and whichever side wins will be master over the other.' The brothers agreed and a time and place were set. It only remained for the Romans and the Albans to make a formal promise that the losing side would accept the rule of the other without argument.

The promise was duly made and, as agreed, the six men took up their weapons. At once both armies began to shout: 'The gods are with you', 'Remember Rome!', 'Curiatii for ever!' The brothers were eager to get started and these shouts encouraged them still further. They came forward into the space between the two armies. Each army was standing in front of its own camp and although they were in no immediate danger their anxiety was plain – the whole future of their lives hung on the courage and luck of a mere handful of men. This was no relaxing spectacle; their nerves were strained and tense.

The trumpet sounded. The brothers moved towards each other

with enough ferocity, discipline and determination for an entire army. No thoughts of personal danger weighed on them, only the knowledge that they alone were to decide their cities' future, as masters or slaves. Metal clashed on metal, swords gleamed in the sunlight. A terrible excitement ran through the watching armies. At first they were quiet, as the brothers matched blow for blow. But soon it turned to close fighting with writhing bodies and swift thrusts of swords and daggers. Now the spectators could see wounds and blood pouring from them. All three Curiatii were hurt, but two of the Romans fell to the ground, one on top of the other, dying.

The Albans screamed in triumph. The Romans' future looked hopeless. In dread their eyes clung to their single champion, surrounded now by his three enemies. Somehow he had come through unscathed. He was still no match for three men together but in single combat his chances were good. With this in mind he took to his heels, knowing they would follow him as fast as their wounds allowed them. He ran on some way, then turned round. The three were widely strung out with the leader not far behind him. The Roman rounded on him furiously. The Alban army were yelling at the other Curiatii to help their brother. But Horatius had already killed him and was confidently waiting for the second encounter. Meanwhile the shouts of encouragement from the Roman side showed that they could hardly believe this change in their luck. Horatius did not keep them waiting. The third of his enemies was not far away. Before he could reach him, Horatius despatched his second opponent and now it was down to single combat. But there was no comparison in their morale and stamina. The Roman was still unhurt and buoyed up with his double victory; his opponent was exhausted from running and loss of blood, and he had seen the fate of both his brothers . . . There was no real contest. From the start he was a beaten man.

Horatius was jubilant. 'I have killed two men in honour of my brothers' memory. This one will settle the war. We Romans are the masters now.' A downward slash broke through the man's wavering guard and pierced his throat. Horatius took the armour off the body and walked back to the Roman ranks, to a storm of cheers and congratulations. The excitement was overwhelming, all the more so because disaster had been so close.

The two armies then marched home, the Romans led by Horatius carrying the spoils of his triple victory. He was met outside the Capena gate by his young sister. She had been engaged to one of the Curiatii and now she saw, on her brother's shoulder, a cloak which had belonged to her fiancé; she herself had made it for him. Letting down her hair she burst into tears and began to call out her dead lover's name. Her wailing, at the moment when every other Roman was cheering her brother's success, struck right at his heart. He drew his sword.

'I see you have no thought for your dead brothers, or me, or Rome', he said. 'Go and join your lover, you and your girlish passion! There shall be no tears for the enemy while I'm alive.' And with these harsh words he drove the sword through her body. The crowd were horrified at this appalling deed. In spite of his recent heroism he was arrested and brought before the king. Tullus realised that by law the verdict must be 'death'. This would certainly be highly unpopular with the mob and he had no intention of passing such a sentence himself. So he called an assembly and said: 'As I am entitled by law, I hereby appoint two *duumvirs** to pass sentence on this man.' The law he was referring to was a savage one. It ran as follows: 'The *duumvirs* have the power to convict on a charge of treason. If the prisoner appeals, the people shall consider the appeal. If the appeal is turned down then the prisoner's head shall be covered and he shall be hanged by a rope from a barren tree. He shall then be whipped whether he hangs inside or outside the city walls.'

So the *duumvirs* were appointed. As far as they could see, the law meant they had no choice but to condemn the prisoner whether he was guilty or not. So one of them announced: 'Publius Horatius, I find you guilty of treason. Lictor,* bind the prisoner's hands.' The officer came forward and was just fastening the chains when the king intervened. He was anxious to be as merciful as he could without breaking the law, so he urged Horatius to appeal. As a result the final decision was now left in the hands of the people.

In making up their minds, they were influenced most of all by the evidence of the prisoner's father. 'My daughter', he said, 'deserved to die. If I didn't think that, I would have done my fatherly duty and punished my son myself. A few hours ago you knew me as the head of a fine family. Don't take the last of my children from me!' He embraced his son and then pointed to the spoils of the Curiatii, fixed in the place now known as the 'Horatian Spears'.

'This is the man', he went on, 'the man you saw entering the city victorious, triumphant. Fellow Romans, can you stand and see him forced under the yoke,* his hands bound, his body lashed

15

into agony? Why, even the men of Alba could hardly bear to watch something so obscene. Lictor, bind the prisoner's hands! After all they have just saved Rome from slavery. Go on, cover the hero's head and hang him from a barren tree! Lash him here, inside the walls – surrounded by the spoils of his enemies; or why not out there, where his enemies are buried? Wherever you take him, reminders of his bravery will stand in the way of such a wicked punishment.'

The old man's tears and Horatius' total fearlessness had their effect. The verdict was 'not guilty'. Personal admiration had more to do with this than any real sense of justice; he *had* murdered his sister and somehow this crime must be paid for. So his father was given a sum of money from public funds to perform some ritual ceremonies that would clear his son's guilt (in fact these ceremonies became a tradition in the family). A wooden beam was put up across the road and Horatius was made to walk underneath it with his head covered, as though he was going under the yoke. This is the origin of the so-called Sister's Beam which the state authorities still renew from time to time. The sister in question was buried where she had been murdered. A monument of shaped stone blocks marked the place.

> Around 625 B.C., Tullus Hostilius died after a reign of some forty-five years. Still the population was growing fast. One result, Livy says, was that 'the difference between right and wrong became rather vague'. The fourth king, Ancus Martius, built Rome's first prison. Another result was that being king of Rome was a prize worth working for – and plotting for.

THE STRUGGLES FOR POWER – I: c.625 B.C.

During Ancus' reign a man called Lucumo arrived in Rome. Rich and energetic, he saw Rome as a promising place to realise his ambitions. He had been unable to spread his wings in his home town, Tarquinii, because he was a foreigner – a Greek in fact, the son of Demaratus of Corinth. But he had inherited all his father's money and was keen to do something with it. His marriage to Tanaquil gave his ambition a further push. She came from a good Etruscan family and fought hard against the truth – that by marrying Lucumo she had moved down the social ladder. The Etruscans despised her husband as the son of a foreign refugee, and such treatment was too much for her pride. Loyalty to her home town of Tarquinii was not as important as seeing her husband held in respect. So she began to think about leaving.

Rome seemed to be the most hopeful place: no ancient families there, everything was young, and 'nobility' was simply the reward for capability. It was just the place for a thrusting, determined man. She easily persuaded Lucumo since he was ambitious and only tied to Tarquinii on his mother's side. They packed and left for Rome.

Their carriage had reached the Janiculum hill when suddenly an eagle came gliding down and snatched the cap off Lucumo's head. It hovered over the carriage with tremendous screeches and squawks before swooping down again like some messenger of the gods and neatly dropping the cap back in place. It then flew off. Like all Etruscans, Tanaquil was an expert at interpreting such signs and this one is said to have left her in the highest spirits. Throwing her arms around Lucumo she said, 'You have a great future ahead of you. The king of birds from that quarter of the sky must be a sign from Jupiter. It came to the highest part of your head, took off your earthly 'crown', only to put it back as a sign that he supports you.' Full of confidence and excitement they drove into Rome. They bought a house and Lucumo changed his name to Lucius Tarquinius Priscus.

As a newcomer, and a rich one, he soon attracted the attention of Roman society. He made the most of this, always ready with a kind word, throwing parties and, where he could, using his money to win friends. Soon his reputation reached the palace. The king began to employ him for official business, on which Tarquinius used his money as well as his brains. Before long he was the king's close friend. Foreign affairs, home affairs, palace affairs, he had a hand in them all, and was so successful that eventually the king even named him in his will as his children's guardian.

Ancus was king for twenty-four years. His reputation both as a wartime leader and as a peacetime administrator could match that of any of the previous kings. When he died his two sons were already verging on manhood, which explains why Tarquinius was in a hurry to have an election for Ancus' successor. A date was set and a few days before it he sent the boys off hunting. It is said that Tarquinius was the first king who owed his throne to his own deliberate efforts. He was the first too who addressed the common people to get them on his side.

'There's nothing unusual', he said, 'in what I am asking. If I was the first foreigner to be king of Rome, then I would expect some of you to be surprised and indignant. As it is, there have been two foreign kings already. Tatius was not only a foreigner but an enemy; as for Numa, he knew nothing about Rome, didn't particularly want to be king and only accepted the throne because he was formally requested to do so. I however came here, with my wife and all my belongings, the very moment I was my own master. In fact I've spent more of my adult life here than in my home town. I've learnt about Roman political laws and Roman military customs in peacetime and in war, learnt from King Ancus himself – quite a reputable teacher! No one has done his duty to the king more conscientiously and no one, not even the king himself, has been more generous to the people of Rome.'

All this was true, and Tarquinius was appointed king by a large majority. Once on the throne this highly able man put the same energy into keeping his power as he had into getting it in the first place. For example, he added a hundred men to the Senate, from then on called the 'junior members'. Certainly this put the Senate on a broader footing but it did no harm to his prospects either. Tarquinius was responsible for appointing these new senators and they were solidly behind him.

STRUGGLES FOR POWER – II: c.600 B.C.

About this time a very strange thing happened in the palace. It had remarkable consequences too. There was a boy living there called Servius Tullius. One day he was asleep when suddenly a crown of flames appeared on his head. A number of people were around at the time and naturally there was considerable uproar at this extraordinary sight. The king and queen came to see what it was all about and one of the slaves arrived with water to put out the flames. But Tanaquil held him back. 'Calm down, all of you!' she said. 'And don't touch the boy! Let him wake up in his own time!' – and when he did, the flames vanished.

Tanaquil then had a private talk with Tarquinius. 'At present this boy is being brought up as a slave. But it's clear that one day, when Rome is in trouble, we shall look to him as our inspiration and strength and then both we and the city will have cause to be proud of him. In the meantime we must look after him as carefully as we can.' So from then on he was treated as one of the family and given an education to fit him for his glorious future. Certainly the gods approved. He grew up to be a true prince and when

Tarquinius was looking for a husband for his daughter he was the obvious choice from all points of view. So he became the king's son-in-law. (From this it seems unlikely he was ever a slave. I tend to believe the story that his mother was a foreign princess captured by the Romans. This would explain the rumour about his slavery.)

Tarquinius remained as king for something like thirty-eight years. By this time he and the senators and the people of Rome all regarded Servius as by far the most distinguished man in the city. Now King Ancus' two sons had always harboured a bitter grudge against Tarquinius for betraying his trust as their guardian and depriving them of their father's kingdom. They thought it was a disgrace for Rome to be ruled by an outsider – and the man was not even an Italian! But now, apparently, they were going to be bypassed once again, this time in favour of a slave. It was too much. A mere hundred years earlier this earthly throne had been occupied by Romulus – a god and the son of a god. And at any moment it might pass into the hands of Servius, a slave and the son of a slave. To think that the road to power lay open to such people while Ancus' own sons were in the prime of life – it was an insult to Rome. Worse, it was a slur on their family name.

They decided to use violence. For several reasons Tarquinius, not Servius, was their target. They wanted revenge first of all, and then if Tarquinius survived to try them he was likely to show less mercy than a private citizen over a charge of murder. In any case, if they killed Servius the king could just choose another son-in-law to succeed him. So Tarquinius it was to be.

They picked two shepherds for the job, the roughest types they could find. These two went to the palace, carrying a variety of ordinary farming implements. When they got to the main hall they pretended to quarrel. This involved the maximum of noise, and the palace slaves closed in on them. By this time they were both shouting 'I demand to see the king', and the row could be heard right through the building. They were in fact summoned into the king's presence, but they went on shouting and arguing until the lictor intervened.

'Silence! Now then, one at a time!' They stopped arguing and one of the shepherds then launched into his made-up story. The king turned to him and listened carefully. As he did so, the other shepherd lifted up an axe and brought it crashing down on his head. Without stopping to pull out the weapon, they were through the door and running.

The king fell dying into the arms of his retinue. The murderers were caught by the lictors and at once there was pandemonium, everyone rushing around, wanting to know what had happened. In the middle of all this, Tanaquil ordered the palace gates to be locked and insisted on being alone with the body. She started busily mixing medicines for the wound, as if the king might actually recover. She also set in motion a long-term plan, for the time when the king's death could not be hidden any longer. She immediately sent for Servius. Tarquinius by now was nearly dead. Tanaquil pointed to the body and clasped Servius by the hand.

'You must avenge the king's death. Do you want to see me jeered at by my enemies? The throne is yours, Servius, if you are man enough to take it. Why should it go to men who hired others to commit this terrible crime for them? Be bold! Go where the gods are leading you! All those years ago they foretold your future with the crown of flames. March forward now with those flames as your banner! Now is the time for action. Tarquinius and I have ruled Rome in spite of our foreign blood. It's your character, not your origin, that matters. If your mind is numbed by the speed of events, at least do as I say!'

Outside, the yelling and pushing of the mob was threatening to get out of hand. The palace in those days was just by the temple of Jupiter the Founder, so Tanaquil went to the windows on the top storey that looked out on the New Road. From here she addressed the crowd.

'There is no cause for alarm. The attack has just left the king in a state of shock. It was not a heavy blow and he's already regained consciousness. We've examined the wound, cleaned away the blood, and there is no serious damage. I'm quite sure that in a few days you'll be seeing him for yourselves. In the meantime I would ask you to put your complete trust in Servius Tullius while he's looking after the king's legal and other duties.'

Servius then adopted all the royal trappings of robes and lictors. When cases were brought to him to decide he settled some straightaway but postponed others, saying he had better ask the king's advice. As the days went by after Tarquinius' death the secret was still closely guarded and the king's 'assistant' was making his own position stronger and stronger. Eventually the time came for the truth to be announced (sounds of mourning could be heard in the palace). Servius made sure he had a reliable bodyguard. He needed it, because he was the first king to have the common people against him. His only support came from the Senate. As for Ancus' two sons, the news had soon reached them that their hired assassins were under arrest, that Tarquinius was alive and Servius totally in control. They immediately left Rome for ever.

To get complete command of Rome, Servius had to act on the private as well as the public front. He was afraid that Tarquinius' two sons, Lucius and Arruns, might plot against him, just as Ancus' sons had done against Tarquinius. His answer was to marry off his two daughters to Tarquinius' sons. But the workings of Fate were too strong for any human to deflect. Soon the whole palace, right down to the slaves, was involved in revolutionary plots of one sort or another.

All this intrigue was stifled for the moment by the timely outbreak of war against Veii, with whom the truce had run out, and against other Etruscan cities. Through a combination of courage and good luck Servius made a name for himself. A large enemy army was utterly routed and by the time he returned to Rome there was no doubt in anyone's mind, whether senator or working man – Servius was king.

STRUGGLES FOR POWER – III: c.550 B.C.

But even though he had made his position secure, Servius knew that Lucius Tarquinius was stirring up trouble behind his back, saying the Romans had never voted to have Servius as their king. First Servius made a move to get the common people on his side: he gave each of them some of the land just captured from the Etruscans. Then he risked holding a referendum. Did they want him as their king or not? With the largest majority ever the answer was 'yes'.

This result did not dampen Lucius' expectations in the slightest. In fact he was more hopeful than ever because he knew that the handout of land had annoyed the Senate. Being young and ambitious he reckoned that by attacking Servius over this he could win some support among the senators. So it was that in Rome, as elsewhere, absolute power led to tragedy. But the hatred of the Roman people for such power made sure this king would be the last: an early reign of terror was to sow the seeds of liberty.

Lucius' brother Arruns was a mild and gentle young man.

Their wives too (Servius' two daughters, as I have already mentioned) were very different in character. For a time fortune favoured Rome in not allowing the two most ruthless of the four to marry each other – Lucius, that is, and Arruns' wife Tullia. This gave Servius a little longer to exert his valuable influence on Roman affairs. Tullia was furious and bitter that her husband showed no interest whatever in carving out a glorious career for himself. She turned her attention to his elder brother. She began to tell him how much she admired him. He was a real man with royal blood in his veins. For her sister she had nothing but contempt: 'You get yourself a husband like that and then you're too feeble to back him up!'

Lucius and Tullia were too alike to stay apart for long. Evil attracts evil. But it was Tullia who set the disturbance in motion. In the course of her secret conversations with Lucius she freely spoke her opinions of his brother and of her own sister:

'We'd be better off if I were a widow and you a bachelor again – anything rather than be tied to these dead weights. If only the gods had given me a husband as forceful as myself! We'd soon have my father off the throne.'

This sort of talk had its effect on Lucius. Two funerals took place, then Lucius and Tullia were married. Even if Servius did not prevent the wedding, he can hardly have been pleased about it.

From that moment the old man's throne and his life were in ever-increasing danger. Tullia soon found that one evil deed leads to another. She could not bear the thought that she had engineered two murders for nothing. As a result Lucius got no peace.

'I wasn't short of a husband to keep me company, quietly, in slavery. I wanted an ambitious one, one who wouldn't forget he was the son of Tarquinius Priscus, one who would rather *be* king than dream about it. If you are really the man I thought you were, then hail, husband and king! If not, then I have made the mistake of marrying a coward as well as a criminal. Stir yourself, Lucius! It isn't as if you have to make your way from Corinth or Tarquinii, like your father, and fight for a throne in a foreign city. You are the king of Rome by right! Wherever you look there are the proofs: the gods of your home and country, your father's statue, his throne, his palace, the very name "Tarquinius". If you haven't the guts for it, why give people false hopes? Why go round acting the prince? I should creep back to Tarquinii or Corinth. It's the common blood coming out in you, as it did in your brother. Your father was made of better stuff.'

This is the kind of bullying he was subjected to. For Tullia, one of the main spurs to action was the queen. Not even born in Rome, by her own efforts Tanaquil had reached a position where she had twice been behind the appointment of a king, first her husband, then her son-in-law. Tullia could not bear the thought that even with the advantage of royal blood she herself should have no say as to who would be king. She drove her husband on like a demon. He began going round the 'junior members' of the Senate and sounding out support. 'It's thanks to my father', he would say, 'that you're in the Senate at all. One good turn deserves another.' Among the younger citizens he found money a useful tool. He was full of promises about all the great things he was going to do and of attacks on all the things Servius was doing wrong. Soon his influence was felt all over Rome.

At last the time came for action. With a solid bodyguard of armed men he marched into the forum. Amid a stunned silence he seated himself on the king's throne in front of the senate-house and addressed the herald: 'Summon all senators to appear in the senate-house before King Tarquinius!'

They assembled with noticeable speed. Some were already in the know. Others were afraid that not to attend might mean a charge of treason – the suddenness of it all was quite breathtaking and certainly it looked as though Servius' days were numbered. Before them in the senate-house Tarquinius launched into a detailed attack on the king, beginning with his family background.

'Gentlemen, the man is a slave, and so was his mother. After my father's brutal murder there was no question of him performing the king's duties just for the time being; no question of elections, or a popular vote, or support from this Senate. He got the throne as a present from his mother-in-law. With that background, it's not surprising he was always on the side of the riffraff, scum like himself. He treated decent people with contempt, like another breed. Look how he stole land from the leading men of Rome and handed it over to the nearest gang of blackguards! Once, the taxes were spread fairly; now you senators have to pay most of them. And that census he organised, that was so that every man of any wealth had to say how much he owned, and become a target for greed and envy. It also meant that when Servius wanted to bribe the poor, he knew where to get the money from.'

23

By now the alarm had reached the king and at this point he burst furiously into the senate-house and immediately shouted, 'What is the meaning of this, Tarquinius? How dare you summon the senators and sit on my throne while I am still alive?'

Tarquinius shouted back, 'This is my father's throne. A king's son has more right here than a mere slave. Your betters have had enough of being cheated and jeered at.'

At this the opposing sides broke into uproar. The mob invaded the senate-house and the battle for the throne began in earnest. Tarquinius had gone too far now to stop at half-measures. He was younger and stronger than the king and picked him up bodily. He carried him out of the senate-house and sent him crashing down the steps to the very bottom. Then he strode back inside to restore order.

Servius' friends and attendants fled for their lives, leaving him to crawl home as best he could. But Tarquinius had sent a band of assassins after him. The king was found and killed. It is more than possible, given Tullia's character, that she was behind her father's murder. At all events we know for a fact that she drove to the forum in her carriage, apparently ignoring the mob that was milling round it, called her husband out of the senate-house, and was the first to hail him as King Tarquinius. He told her to keep away from the violence and go home. She started off and reached the top of Cyprus Street, where the temple of Diana used to be until quite recently. There the coachman turned right, heading for the Urbian slope and then the Esquiline hill. Suddenly he dragged the horses to a standstill, in terror. He pointed ahead, to where Servius' butchered corpse lay in the roadway. That street is still called the Street of Sin, and it takes its name from the foul, inhuman crime that followed. Tormented by the avenging spirits of her dead husband and sister, Tullia herself drove the carriage over her father's body. The old man's blood spattered over her and the whole carriage – a stain of guilt that she carried right into the home she shared with Tarquinius. And the gods of that home were angry. They were to lead the new reign from its violent beginnings to an equally violent and sudden end.

THE LAST KING: 532 B.C.

So Lucius Tarquinius became king. His behaviour soon got him the nickname 'Tarquinius the Proud'. Even though the old king had been his father-in-law he refused to allow him a decent burial. 'Remember' he kept on saying, 'no one ever buried Romulus!' He also thought some of the leaders of the Senate had supported Servius against him, and had them murdered. He had given a clear demonstration of what a mixture of crime and ambition could do. It did not take him very long to realise that the same tactics could be used against himself. So wherever he went he was surrounded by soldiers. As he had made himself king without consulting the people or the Senate, this bodyguard was rather appropriate. Brute force was the only thing he could rely on – 'since they won't love me, let them fear me'.

But whatever his political crimes, there is no denying his gifts as a general. His fame in this field might well have equalled that of earlier kings if only people could have forgotten what sort of man he was. He started the long war against the Volsci (it went on for another two hundred years after his death) and captured the city of Suessa Pometia from them. The booty was sold and raised forty talents of silver. This gave Tarquinius the idea of a large-scale project. The forty talents went into a fund for building a magnificent temple to Jupiter, a fitting monument to the king of gods and men, to the power of Rome and, not least, to the splendid site he had chosen.

His next campaign was against the nearby town of Gabii. But here things did not go as planned. First a frontal attack failed, then a blockade. The Romans were even driven away from the town walls. Finally Tarquinius resorted to that most un-Roman of approaches: low cunning. He pretended he had given up the campaign, and that all his energies had turned to getting the foundations of the temple laid, and to other building jobs in the city. Now Tarquinius had three sons. The next stage of the plan was in the hands of Sextus, the youngest, who 'escaped' to Gabii, complaining bitterly of the way his father had been treating him:

'I can't stand his cruelty any longer. The tyrant has turned on his own family now, there are too many children around for his liking. He's turned the Senate into a cemetery; the palace is next on the list. He's determined not to leave anyone to be his successor. His men were out to kill me but I escaped. As far as I can see, the one place I shall be safe is among my father's enemies. Make no mistake! He's not forgotten about the campaign, for all his pretending. He's just biding his time to catch you off your guard. But perhaps you have no mercy to show an exile like me. Then I'll go round the whole of Latium, the Volsci, the Aequi, the Hernici –

I'll find some tribe who can protect a son from his father's unnatural cruelty. Who knows? Maybe I'll find someone prepared to fight against this man's pride and his people's aggression.'

The men of Gabii realised that if they dismissed him he would be angry and would only go off and vent these feelings elsewhere. So they gave him a polite reception.

'We're not surprised', said one of their spokesmen, 'at the way his murderous tendencies have progressed. First the people, then his friends, now his children. In the end he'll only have suicide left! But we're glad you've come to us, Sextus Tarquinius. We hope and believe that with your help we can turn defence into attack'.

Sextus became a member of the council. When they discussed local matters he took care to agree with the most experienced members who knew about these things. He concentrated on stirring up war.

'After all', he said, 'it's the one area I'm expert in. I know the strength of both sides and you can be sure that if even Tarquinius' children can't stand him any longer, then there's little love for him among the Roman public.'

Gradually the leaders of Gabii came round to his way of thinking. He encouraged them by leading some of the toughest young soldiers in raids on Roman territory. Everything he said, everything he did, was aimed at getting the trick to work, and his reputation, false as it was, began to grow. At last, he was appointed to lead the army against Rome.

Still Sextus was the only one who knew what was really happening. Several skirmishes took place between the two sides and Gabii generally managed to win. This convinced everybody in the town, rich and poor, that Sextus Tarquinius had been sent from heaven to be their general. The common soldiers adored him. He was with them through every danger and discomfort and was noticeably generous with his rewards. In short he now ruled Gabii as completely as his father ruled Rome.

From this strong position he was ready to embark on the next stage of the plan. One of his supporters went to Rome to find out what Tarquinius had in mind, now that the gods had delivered Gabii into his son's power. For some reason Tarquinius must have had his doubts as to whether the messenger could be trusted. At any rate he refused to reply to the man's questions. Instead he put on a thoughtful expression and wandered out into the palace garden, followed by his son's messenger. Still he said absolutely nothing. But he began to knock the heads off the poppies with his stick. By this time the messenger had had enough of asking questions only to be ignored, so he went back to Gabii to tell Sextus that his mission had failed. He recounted every detail of his visit, but still could not be sure why the king had refused to say anything – was he in a rage for some reason, or did he have a grudge against Sextus? Or was it just a typical example of his bloody-mindedness?

Sextus, though, had no trouble putting words to his father's pantomime. One by one he began to get rid of the leading citizens of Gabii. Some were publicly tried and convicted, some were easy to dispose of because they were unpopular. In general Sextus did not bother to disguise what he was doing. In one or two cases he was rather more discreet, where those involved were simply too honest to be accused of anything. Others were allowed to escape or were forcibly deported. But whether they were dead or merely elsewhere, everything they possessed was collected into a central fund and then given by Sextus to his favourites. Benefiting as they did from this system of wholesale bribery, they managed to turn a blind eye to the danger that threatened their city as a whole. With no leaders and no allies, it was not long before Gabii passed peacefully into Tarquinius' hands.

> Tarquinius was said to have been much concerned with the physical appearance of Rome, building, among other things, the great temple to Jupiter, Juno and Minerva, and the Cloaca Maxima. This was a great ditch which drained the swampy land at the foot of the Capitol* which then became the forum. It was later roofed over in stone and the surface paved. The system of sewers, of which it formed the backbone, was regarded as one of Rome's greatest achievements. Where it entered the Tiber the Cloaca Maxima was ten feet (3 m) wide and twelve feet (4 m) high: it still forms part of the modern city's drainage system.

The oracle: c.510 B.C.

In the middle of all this activity an ominous thing happened. A snake came sliding out of one of the wooden pillars in the palace. Everyone scattered in terror, except the king. He wasn't so much afraid of the snake as alarmed about what this sign meant. Until now, when some sign like this was sent to the Roman people, they had always turned to Etruscan soothsayers*. But Tarquinius was

27

so terrified to have this happening inside his own home that he decided he must consult the most famous of all oracles*, at Delphi. The oracle's reply was too important to be entrusted to just anybody. So Sextus' two elder brothers, Titus and Arruns, were chosen to make the journey to Greece. This meant travelling over then uncharted territory and a sea voyage that was indeed a voyage into the unknown.

The two brothers duly left and took with them their cousin Lucius Junius Brutus, son of the king's sister Tarquinia. Now he was in fact a very different man from what he seemed to be. His own brother had been one of the leading citizens liquidated by Tarquinius. As a result he had made up his mind about two things: he must not alarm the king by his behaviour, and he must not possess anything the king might take a fancy to. Where justice had ceased to exist, Tarquinius' contempt was the best protection. So he pretended to be an idiot. When the king took over all his property, he did not complain. He even put up with the nickname Brutus, the Blockhead. Under the cover of this insult the guardian of Rome's freedom could quietly bide his time. His cousins had brought him along not as a friend, but more as a stooge for their jokes. But the story goes that as his gift to Apollo he took a hollow stick with a rod of gold inside – like himself, dull on the surface.

They all arrived at Delphi and the two brothers got the oracle's answer to their father's questions about the snake. But they couldn't resist asking one further question: 'Which one of us will be the next king of Rome?' From the depths of the cave came the answer:

> 'Young men, consider this upon your journey home,
> The first to kiss his mother shall be great in Rome.'

They all swore to keep this answer a secret. Sextus had been left behind in the palace and his brothers were determined he should know nothing about it, and so have no chance of becoming king. As to who should kiss their mother first when they got back, they decided this by drawing lots. Brutus however reckoned that the oracle had meant something quite different. He pretended to trip over and in doing so touched the earth with his mouth – because, as you know, the earth is the mother of us all. So they returned safely to Rome, where they found everyone hard at work getting ready for war.

Lucretia

The campaign was aimed at the Rutuli and their city, Ardea. For an Italian tribe of that period the Rutuli were particularly wealthy, which was all the reason Tarquinius needed. For one thing he wanted to recoup some of the private fortune he had spent on his extravagant building programme. For another he needed something to soothe the mob, and money would do very nicely. They hated Tarquinius anyway – he was that sort of man – but by treating them for so long as slaves and labourers he had brought their hatred to a new pitch.

A direct attack on Ardea failed. So it would have to be blockaded. The usual digging began and the Roman army settled into a permanent camp. Obviously it was going to be a war needing patience rather than heroics, so it was fairly easy, especially for the senior officers, to get leave. The young princes also staved off boredom with a number of drunken parties. One day they were all drinking as guests of Sextus Tarquinius. Collatinus, Sextus' second cousin, was also there, when the conversation got round to wives. Each one was quick to say what a truly remarkable wife he had and before long they were all arguing furiously, when Collatinus interrupted:

'Gentlemen, why are we wasting our breath? It would only take a few hours to put our theories to the test – and prove that my Lucretia is the best of all! Those of you who are men enough, ride back to Rome with me and let's see for ourselves what sort of wives we have. There's nothing like a surprise visit for revealing the truth!'

In their drunken state they all jumped at the idea and were soon galloping towards Rome. They reached the city just as dusk was falling. And every princess was found in the middle of an extravagant dinner-party with her friends. Finally they rode on to Collatia. By now it was late evening, but Lucretia was still sitting in her room spinning by lamplight, with her maids busy all round her. There was no doubt, she was the winner of the contest. She greeted her husband and his friends warmly and Collatinus celebrated his victory by inviting the young princes to supper. At that supper Sextus was first fired with passion for Lucretia. She was so beautiful and so pure, as they had seen that evening . . . But when supper was over that was the end of their night-time adventure. They all returned to camp.

Sextus waited a few days. Then, without telling Collatinus, he took one companion and came back to Collatia. Lucretia greeted him with a smile and offered him supper. Obviously no one in the house knew what was in Sextus' mind and after supper he was escorted to the guest wing. By now he was nearly crazy with lust. At last everything was quiet; surely everyone was asleep? He drew his sword and made his way to the bedroom where Lucretia lay. As he put his left hand on her breast he whispered: 'Don't speak, Lucretia. It's Sextus Tarquinius. And I've got a sword in my right hand. One word and you die . . .' In those first few moments of panic she realised she was helpless in the face of death. And now Sextus began to tell her how passionately he loved her, pleading, begging, threatening, trying somehow to win her over. But she refused to give way. So then, seeing that the fear of death by itself was not enough, he added to his threats: 'I can destroy your honour as well as your life; I just kill one of your slaves, strip him and lay him next to your dead body. "She paid the penalty for her filthy crime", they'll say.'

At that, she gave in to him. Tarquinius rode off, gloating at his triumph. Lucretia in her distress sent a message to her father in Rome and to her husband in Ardea: 'Come quickly, and bring someone you can trust. Something terrible has happened.' Her father arrived with Publius Valerius, Volesus' son, and her husband with Brutus – these two were in fact already on their way to Rome when they got the message. They found Lucretia distraught, sitting in her room. As they came through the door she burst into tears.

'Are you well?' asked Collatinus.

'What woman can be well when she has lost her honour? Another man, Collatinus, has known the pleasures of your bed. But, as death is my witness, it is only my body that has been unfaithful, my heart is innocent. Swear now, and promise that the criminal shall not escape his punishment. Sextus Tarquinius is the man. Last night I received him as a guest in the house. And he repaid me with armed assault. Then he took his pleasure at my expense – and at his own too, if you are men of honour.'

They each gave their promise and tried to comfort her:

'You are innocent. Sextus is the one who is guilty.'

'A body can't sin by itself – only a mind can sin.'

'You were forced to give in. That's no crime.'

To these words she replied: 'You will deal with Sextus as you think best. Maybe I am innocent. But, in my eyes, I must still be punished. I cannot bear the thought that in the future any unfaithful wife should escape death by pleading "Lucretia did not die." ' With these words she took a knife from the folds of her dress and plunged it into her heart. As she fell forward, dying, her husband and father cried out in horror. But while they sobbed with grief, Brutus pulled the knife from Lucretia's body. He held it out in front of him, still dripping with blood:

'This blood was the purest in Rome, till Tarquinius polluted it. And by this blood I swear an oath – hear me, you gods in heaven: I swear that by the sword, by fire, in whatever way I can, I shall pursue Lucius Tarquinius Superbus, and his foul wife, and all his brood. Never again, while I live, shall they or any other man be king in Rome.'

The knife passed to Collatinus, then to Lucretius and Valerius. They were struck dumb by his behaviour. This was not the Brutus they knew. But they repeated his oath and as they did so their grief turned to anger. Brutus was calling for instant revolution – they were his to command.

They took Lucretia's body from the house and laid it out in the forum of Collatia. As you might expect, a crowd soon gathered to express its amazement and horror. They were shocked at the violence of Sextus' crime, and full of sympathy for Lucretia's father, but Brutus interrupted their murmurings: 'Tears and complaints won't get us anywhere. What we need are true Romans who will dare to fight these tyrants.'

The toughest of the townsmen answered his call at once and the rest soon followed. Brutus left Lucretia's father to hold Collatia and posted guards to stop anyone slipping out and warning the king or his family. Then he led the rest of the men off in the direction of Rome.

In Rome the appearance of this armed force caused considerable panic wherever it went. A second look, however, showed that it was led by several of the city's most responsible citizens, so clearly, whatever it was, it was not just a mob looking for trouble. As in Collatia, word soon got round and reaction to the tragic story was just as strong. Before long there was a large crowd in the forum. Now as it happened Brutus was at that time the tribune of the king's bodyguard. Using this position as justification, the official herald therefore called on the people to listen to Brutus' speech.

It was not the sort of speech they expected from the Blockhead. His themes were the violent, disgusting behaviour of Sextus, his unspeakable crime against Lucretia, her terrible death, and her father's bereavement. Bad enough to have lost a daughter, but how much worse and more degrading was the reason for her death!

'And then' he went on, 'there's the overbearing attitude of King Tarquinius. To think of the hours you've spent sweating in ditches and underground sewers; you, men of Rome, who have proved yourselves the masters of every town round about, now back in civilian life as workmen and stone-cutters! And let us not ignore the ugly way our last king met his end – and how his treacherous daughter drove her carriage over his body. May the avenging gods not forget that!'

No doubt, in his anger, he reminded them of other, worse crimes. But there is no need for a historian to dwell on these. In any case, the effect on the crowd was electric. In a moment they were yelling 'Down with the king!' and 'Tyrants OUT!' Brutus took some armed volunteers to stir up mutiny in the army outside Ardea. He left Rome in the charge of Lucretius, who had in fact already been appointed city prefect* by Tarquinius. In the middle of all this uproar the queen fled from the palace. Wherever she went men and women screamed curses at her and prayed to the gods to punish her crime.

The news soon reached the king at Ardea. In a panic he set out for Rome to put down the rebellion. Brutus realised this might happen, so he took a side road to bypass the king's forces. He reached Ardea about the same time Tarquinius reached Rome.

Tarquinius found the gates of Rome closed – he was no longer wanted there. But Brutus, as the saviour of Rome, got a tremendous reception from the army. They sent the king's sons packing and two of them went into exile with their father in Caere, a town in Etruria. Sextus actually went off to Gabii as if he owned the place. But his reign of terror had left bitter memories, and he was soon assassinated.

Lucius Tarquinius Superbus had been king for twenty-five years. Two hundred and forty-four years passed from the founding of Rome by Romulus to its liberation by Brutus. The Romans now held an election, following the voting methods organised by Servius Tullius. And as a result, the city prefect appointed two consuls: Brutus and Collatinus.

2 The early republic

The new republic had not seen the last of Tarquinius. Under his rule the young men of Rome had lived lives of luxury, and they tried to restore him to the throne. The plot was discovered and the traitors executed, among them Brutus' two sons. Then Tarquinius attacked Rome, but was defeated. However Brutus was killed in the battle, which possibly raised Tarquinius' hopes. He was still determined to get his throne back somehow.

TARQUINIUS RETURNS: 506 B.C.

The attack

For the time being Tarquinius and his family had found a home with Lars Porsenna, the king of Clusium in Etruria. In return they treated him to a regular flow of requests and advice:

'We are Etruscans too, of the same blood as yourself. Are you going to allow us to stay in exile as beggars? This habit of expelling kings seems to be growing. It's not a thing you should ignore. The word "liberty" has a nice sound to it. We must fight to stamp out its dangerous attraction. Otherwise everyone will end up together, at the bottom of the heap; there'll be no authority anywhere, no one to look up to. So much for monarchy, the finest thing in heaven or on earth.'

Porsenna realised that having a king in Rome made life safer for the Etruscans, still more so if that king was himself an Etruscan. So he raised an army to attack Rome. The strength of Clusium and Porsenna's reputation led to unheard-of scenes of panic in the Senate. But this was not all the senators had to worry about. They had no confidence at all in the support of the Roman mob. Once fear spread among them, they might open the gates to Tarquinius and put up with slavery just to get peace. So the Senate decided to bribe them. Corn was the first thing: trade missions were sent to the Volsci and to Cumae. Then there was the question of the salt monopoly: this belonged to private speculators and the price had risen, so now the state took it over. Finally, the burden of taxes

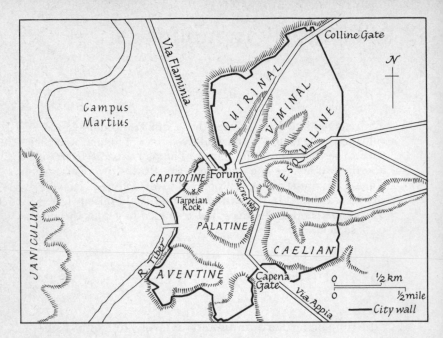

Early Rome

and tolls was shifted to those who could afford it. All the poor had
to do for Rome was produce children.

The Senate's generosity paid off. There was no split even when,
later on, the blockade led to hunger and appalling con-
ditions inside the city. Tarquinius had no supporters even among
the poorest. In later years there were men who tricked their way
into becoming so-called 'popular' leaders, but none of them was
as really popular as the Senate at this time, thanks to its sensible
policies.

The Etruscans advanced on Rome and the local farmers fled
into the city to save themselves. With guards, walls and the Tiber
to protect it, it seemed safe enough, but the enemy almost found a
way in over the pontoon bridge. Only one man prevented them,
Horatius Cocles. He was Rome's defence in her hour of need. He
happened to be on guard at the bridge and from here he saw the
Etruscans suddenly attack the Janiculum hill, on the other side of
the river, and capture it. Then they came rushing down the slope
opposite him. In front of them came a terrified mob of Roman
soldiers, in no sort of order, even throwing away their weapons so
they could run faster. Horatius grabbed them one by one, as they

came past. He tried to stand in their way, begging them to respect their oaths to the gods and their loyalty to Rome.

'What's the point of running' he shouted, 'if you don't block the way in? If they cross this bridge, there'll soon be more Etruscans in Rome than outside. You must smash the bridge behind me, cut it down, burn it, anything. I'll hold them off as well as I can.'

He then rushed to the Janiculum side of the bridge. He stood out clearly among the mass of fleeing bodies. As he prepared for the coming fight, the Etruscans stared at him in amazement – such courage was unbelievable. But two of the Romans near him were shamed by his bravery. Spurius Lartius and Titus Herminius were noblemen and outstanding fighters. For a short time they helped Horatius to repel the first and fiercest attacks. Then the men smashing the bridge behind them began to call them back. There was very little of it left, and Horatius made his companions retire to safety.

Now he turned a furious look on the ranks of Etruscans. He began to taunt them, now and then picking on one in particular as a target for his insults.

'Your proud kings treat you like dirt. You've obviously forgotten what freedom's like. Otherwise you wouldn't be here trying to crush ours.'

For a few minutes they hesitated; looked round to see if anyone else was going to charge. Finally pride won the day. With a shout, they all began hurling spears at their lone enemy. But his shield protected him from all their attacks. Still he stood firmly on the bridge. Now they tried to dislodge him with a charge. Suddenly, there was a rending crash of wood and a shout from the Romans – the bridge had been destroyed in time! The Etruscan advance petered out.

Horatius then raised his voice: 'Father Tiber, I pray to your holy name. May your waters receive kindly this soldier and his armour.' So, fully armed, he jumped into the Tiber. Spears flew thick about him, but he swam to the Roman side unharmed. Everyone in the years to come would remember what he had done, incredible though his bravery might sound.

Rome showed her gratitude to the hero. A statue of him was put up near the forum, and he was given as much land as he could plough round in a day. Private citizens too were quick to show their admiration. In the food shortage that followed, many of them brought him supplies that they could ill afford to do without.

Rome surrounded

With the failure of his direct attack, Porsenna now settled down to a blockade. As this went on, food in Rome became expensive and scarce. Porsenna's hopes rose of starving the city into defeat. But one young nobleman, called Gaius Mucius was angry at this state of affairs. When Rome had been ruled by kings, no enemy had ever dared to blockade it; now it was 'free', it was surrounded by Etruscans, whom the Romans had beaten many a time in the past. Mucius felt some bold gesture was called for, something to restore Rome's prestige and morale. First he thought of making a solo expedition to the Etruscan camp. But then he realised it would be dangerous to do this on his own without the consuls' permission – if the Roman guards caught him he would be arrested as a deserter. And, in the present state of things, it would be a plausible charge. So he went to the Senate.

'Gentlemen', he said, 'I want to cross the Tiber and, if possible, get into the Etruscan camp. It's not money I'm after, and not revenge either. But, with the gods' help, something more important altogether.'

The senate gave its permission and Mucius set off, with a dagger hidden under his tunic. He reached the camp and mingled with a large crowd milling round the platform where the king was sitting. It happened to be the soldiers' pay-day. On the platform with the king was his secretary. His uniform was much the same as the king's and he was very busy answering the soldiers' questions. Now obviously Mucius could not ask anyone 'Excuse me, which one is Porsenna?' He would be suspected straight away. So he guessed. And stabbed the wrong one.

Waving the bloodstained dagger he carved a way through the terrified crowd. But their shouts brought the king's bodyguard in force. They caught Mucius and dragged him back to face Porsenna. Although he had failed, and now had little to hope for, Mucius moved straight into the attack.

'I am a citizen of Rome. My name is Gaius Mucius. I came here to kill you. But if I'm to die instead, well, I'm ready for that too. We Romans are fighters, but we can suffer if we have to. Don't think, though, that I'm the only one who will make the attempt. There are plenty more after me just waiting for the honour. So prepare yourself, Porsenna, if you will. Every hour of every day, your life is in danger. Maybe there's even a Roman soldier waiting in your bedroom . . . That's the kind of war you can expect from the warriors of Rome. You needn't worry about pitched battles any more. Just about yourself, and one of us.'

Porsenna was furious as well as frightened.

'You're going to explain every detail of these vague threats, now. Otherwise I shall have you burnt alive.'

'I am one of those who put honour before mere flesh. If you don't believe me, then watch!'

A fire had been lit on the altar for a sacrifice. Mucius plunged his right hand into the flames and held it there. He showed no sign of pain. The king could hardly believe what he saw. Jumping up, he ordered his guards to drag Mucius from the altar.

'You are free to go', he said. 'You have done more harm to yourself than you have to me. If you had showed courage like that while fighting for us, then I should be decorating you for bravery. As it is, I give you an official safe-conduct back to Rome.'

Mucius replied with every appearance of being grateful:

'I see you are a man who appreciates courage. Although you didn't get any information from me by force, I'll tell you this as a favour: there are three hundred of us, young men from the best families in Rome, and we have sworn to kill you, as I said. I drew the first lot. The rest will follow, each in his own good time. And one day your luck will fail.'

So Mucius came back home. From his injury he got the nickname Scaevola, the Left-Handed. And he was soon followed by representatives from Porsenna. The king was far from happy. Only a mistake had saved him from assassination and the thought of all those others waiting for him . . . He was now offering the Romans peace. One of the terms of the treaty he put forward was that Tarquinius should return as king of Rome. He knew the Romans would refuse (and they did) but he felt that in the circumstances he at least had to ask. There were two other points: first, the Romans must give back the land they had taken from Veii and second, if they wanted the Etruscans off the Janiculum hill, then they must allow them to take some Roman hostages. The Romans agreed on both these points. So Porsenna took his army off the Janiculum hill and out of Roman territory. The Senate rewarded Mucius with a plot of land on the other side of the Tiber, later known as Mucius' Meadow.

The young man's success inspired even the Roman women. One of the girls given to the Etruscans as a hostage was called Cloelia. The camp where she was held happened to be within easy reach of the far bank of the Tiber. She managed to lead a group of the other girls past the guards and together they dived into the river. Spears hurtled round them but they all got back safely to their families in Rome.

When Porsenna was told, he was extremely angry. He sent a demand to Rome to have Cloelia back; he didn't care about the rest. But then his admiration gradually got the better of him. He sent a second message: 'What this girl did puts both Horatius and Mucius in the shade. Even so, if you do not send her back, I shall still regard the treaty as broken. But if you do, I promise to return her unharmed.'

Both sides kept their word. The Romans sent her back, according to the terms of the treaty. And Porsenna treated her well, in fact with great respect. 'You can take a number of the other hostages back with you', he told her. 'You choose the ones you would like.' So they were all paraded in front of her. Apparently, being a modest girl, she selected a group of the youngest boys. What is more, all the hostages agreed to this because these boys seemed likely to suffer most from being kept prisoner. The war was now over. Cloelia had shown a new side to the female character and the Romans invented a new form of honour to celebrate the fact. At the top of the Sacred Way they put a statue of her, on horseback.

> Over the next dozen years, fighting between Rome and her neighbours continued. But the most important event was probably the death of Tarquinius in 496. With him out of the way, the plebeians were no longer afraid of anyone becoming king. The patricians now began to seem less like protectors and more like masters. Most of all, the plebeians were angry at the law which forced men who could not pay their debts to become slaves. So, although Rome kept winning on the battlefield, it looked as if a popular revolution was only too likely. Indeed, because the common soldiers fought so bravely, some of the patricians felt sorry for them. Manlius Valerius, appointed Dictator to cope with Rome's military problems, even resigned in disgust at the way they were being treated.

THE BELLY AND THE LIMBS: 494 B.C.

The Senate could see trouble ahead. Once the army was disbanded, the previous plots and secret meetings would start all over again. Now although it was the Dictator who had organised the raising of the army, the soldiers had actually sworn an oath to obey the consuls. The Senate thought this oath would probably keep them in line. So they spread the news that the Aequi were on the warpath. At once the army was under orders to leave Rome.

This was what sparked off the military revolt. One of the rebels' first ideas was to murder the consuls and get out of their oath like that; until, very sensibly, it was pointed out that committing a crime was no way to get round the gods. Eventually a man called Sicinius persuaded them to ignore the consuls and remove themselves to the Sacred Hill. This stands on the other side of the river Anio, about three miles from Rome. They had no official leader, but they put up a wall of earth round their camp and sat quiet. They had taken nothing out of Rome except what food they needed. For several days they just stayed there. They caused no trouble and no one did anything to upset them.

Meanwhile the city was in complete panic. Everything came to a standstill. Without the army to protect them, the rest of the plebeians were terrified the Senate would turn violent. The senators too were frightened, and could not make up their minds whether to expel the rest of the plebeians or not. How long would the deserters stay quiet? And suppose some other tribe declared war? The only hope was to get both parties back together again. No matter what laws were broken, somehow they had to have peace in Rome.

A spokesman would have to go and talk to the plebeians. For this job, the Senate chose Menenius Agrippa. He had a way with words, and the plebeians liked him because he had been born one of them. They let him into the camp and he proceeded to tell them the following story – nothing very subtle, but then speeches tended to be simple in those days:

'Once upon a time, the different parts of the human body were not all in agreement, as they are now. Instead, each bit made up its own mind, had its own opinion. And it seemed very unfair to the other parts of the body that they should worry and sweat away to look after the belly. After all, the belly just sat there in the middle, doing nothing, enjoying all the nice things that came along. So they hatched a plot. The hands weren't going to take food to the mouth; even if they did, the mouth wasn't going to accept it; even if it did, the teeth weren't going to chew it. They went into a sulk and waited for the belly to cry for help. But while they waited, one by one all the parts of the body got weaker and weaker. The moral of this story? The belly too has its job to do. It has to be fed, but it also does feeding of its own. Supported by the food it receives, it sends blood through the system of veins to all the other parts of the body. That blood gives us our health and strength.'

The mutineers took the point, that the revolt of the limbs against the belly matched their own revolt against the Senate. Negotiations began. From these the plebeians got a promise that they could have officials to represent them in the Senate, and these officials were to be protected by the most solemn oaths. Men of the senatorial class could not be chosen and the officials were to be known as 'tribunes of the people'. The first two, Licinius and Albinus, chose three more. Among these was Sicinius, who had led the revolt.

CORIOLANUS, FAMOUS AND INFAMOUS: 494 – 493 B.C.

In their next campaign, the Romans launched a powerful attack on the town of Corioli. Among the Roman officers was a young nobleman called Gaius Marcius, who was later given the honorary name Coriolanus. For all his youth, he was tough and resourceful. He happened to be on guard at a crucial moment in the campaign. The Roman army was ranged all round Corioli and their attention was focused on those shut up inside the walls. The last thing they expected was an attack from outside, but some Volscian troops from Antium came up from the rear. At the same time a force rushed out of Corioli, catching the Romans between two fires.

Marcius collected a body of the toughest soldiers, drove this force back into the town, and pressed on after them through the open gate. Here he laid about him with his sword and seized his chance to set fire to the buildings nearest the wall. The sudden realisation that disaster had struck the town produced, as you may well imagine, a mixture of yells and screams with the howling of women and children; a cheering sound for the Romans, but it knocked the heart out of the relieving force to find their efforts were too late. So they scattered, and Corioli was taken.

Next year Rome was free of wars and there were no political disturbances. Instead she suffered something much worse. When the plebeians had walked out of Rome, the crops had been left with no one to look after them. As a result, the price of grain now began to soar. Then came famine – from the state of things you would have thought Rome was under siege. The slaves and the poorer people were facing starvation.

The consuls took action. They sent dealers along the coast to various parts of Italy to buy corn: north to Etruria, south to the Volsci and on to Cumae, even as far as Sicily. These long journeys had to be made because relations with the tribes all around were so bad. The dealers managed to buy corn at Cumae, but then the town's overlord Aristodemus stepped in. He was an heir of the Tarquinius family. He confiscated the ships full of corn as compensation for his family property taken by the Romans. From the Volsci and the marshy district to the south the dealers could buy nothing at all; not only that, but they went in fear of their lives. Starvation was prevented only by supplies coming down the Tiber from Etruria.

The following year a large shipment of corn arrived from Sicily. Then began a serious discussion in the Senate as to what price the plebeians should pay for it. To many of the senators this seemed the perfect opportunity to put the plebeians in their place: a chance for the Senate to get back the power which they had been blackmailed and bullied into giving away. Of all the tribunes' opponents, one of the most outspoken was Marcius Coriolanus:

'If they want their grain at the old price, then they can give the Senate back its control. Why should I put up with plebeians as magistrates, and Sicinius as one of them? Am I a prisoner of war? Have I been rescued from some band of robbers? This insulting nonsense has gone on long enough. We got rid of King Tarquinius: now Sicinius is lording it over us. Well he can walk out any time, and take the rabble with him. There's a clear road to the Sacred Hill and any other high point he fancies. And if they want food, they can steal it from our land, as they did two years ago. As to the price of grain, they must just put up with it. It's their own fault for going off in a huff. But I don't think we're in for any more armed walkouts, I think they've learnt their lesson. We'll soon see them back on the land, working.'

Maybe Coriolanus was right. It is not easy to say. What I *do* think is that the Senate only had to reduce the price of grain. Then they could have abolished the tribunes and got back all the other various powers they had been forced to give away.

Even the senators thought Coriolanus' speech took too much of a hard line. When the plebeians heard about it, there was almost a revolution on the spot. Starvation stared them in the face, and

41

here they were, being tricked out of their food. One moment, the gods suddenly provided them with corn from across the sea; the next, it was being snatched out of their mouths. The only way out was to give in to Coriolanus, to say farewell to the tribunes, to show him that they were well and truly cowed. In their eyes he had become a bloodsucking monster. What a choice he offered them! Death or slavery.

When he came down the steps from the senate-house there was nearly bloodshed. But the tribunes promptly summoned him to appear before them and this calmed the mob down. Each of them could feel now that Coriolanus was his personal prisoner. Each one of them held this public enemy's life in his hands. Coriolanus' first reaction to the summons was to show his contempt:

'Your job is to help people, not punish them. Anyway, you are tribunes of the people. Senators are outside your control.'

But the mood of the people was very ugly indeed. It looked as though, to save the rest of the senators, Coriolanus would have to be sacrificed. Privately and publicly, they did what they could to help him. To begin with, they sent people round to various individuals to threaten them with violence if they went to any more political meetings. This attempt to cool the situation failed. Then the senators themselves held an open-air meeting. Senators – from the way they behaved, you would have thought they were criminals being tried. Begging, pleading with the people:

'If you must find him guilty, then guilty let him be! But, please, give him to us to deal with. After all, he's only one citizen, one senator out of so many!'

The day for the trial came. Coriolanus did not appear. At that, any idea of pardoning him was forgotten. In his absence he was found guilty of treason and exiled. He went to join the Volsci, full of angry threats against his native city.

Exile: 491 B.C.

The Volsci gave Coriolanus a friendly reception. In fact the longer he stayed, breathing fire and fury against the Romans, the more popular he became. He was staying with Attius Tullius, by some way the most powerful man in local affairs, and a firm enemy of the Romans. What with Tullius' long hatred and Coriolanus' more recent bitterness, it was not long before they began plotting a war against Rome. But the Volsci had been

42

beaten so many times, it was going to be very hard to get them to try yet again. After a long series of campaigns the army had lost men in a serious epidemic. Their morale was shattered. The two men would have to think up some scheme to stir the old feelings of hatred and get the Volsci to begin a new war.

Their chance came when the Romans decided to hold the Great Games for a second time (the first time, the ceremony had gone wrong and Jupiter was angry). The Senate ordered that no expense should be spared. A large contingent of the Volsci came as visitors – this was Tullius' idea. He now followed the plan that he and Coriolanus had worked out. Before the Games started he went to see the consuls.

'There's something affecting public security . . . Could we talk about it in private?' The attendants were sent out of the room, and Tullius went on: 'It's about the Volsci. I'm just anxious to avoid trouble. I'm not saying they've done anything wrong, yet, but I've come to warn you that possibly they might. I have to admit that we're a hot-headed lot. A look at our war record will tell you that! No thanks to ourselves we still survive. We owe that to your generosity. Well, there are a lot of the Volsci here today. And, with the Games on, your people will have their attention distracted. I haven't forgotten the story of the Sabine women. I'm appalled to think of something stupid happening in the heat of the moment. I thought I ought to come and see you first. After all, it's your business as well as ours. As for me, I'm off home as soon as I can. If there *are* fights and quarrels, then I want no part of them.'

When he had gone, the consuls held a meeting with the rest of the senators. There was no real information they could pass on, but they reckoned Tullius would not have come to see them without good reason. So they took his warning seriously. Even without hard facts to go on they preferred, reasonably enough, to be on the safe side. They passed a motion asking the Volsci to leave Rome. The news was announced officially and the deadline set for nightfall. Immediately there was panic, with people rushing around collecting their belongings from wherever they were staying. Then they started to leave. They were slowly recovering from the shock and now the first signs of anger showed themselves. They began to think about how they had been treated. Were they criminals? Did they carry some disease? Were they unfit to attend games and festivals, indeed to have any contact with men and gods?

Soon a long and almost unbroken line of people stretched along the road out of the city. Tullius had gone on ahead to wait for them by the source of the river Ferentina. As the leading citizens arrived he had a private word with each of them. How dare the Romans treat them like this – it was outrageous! Being furious themselves they were quite happy to listen to him, and with their help he collected the rest of the crowd in a field down below the road. He addressed his audience:

'Forget, if you like, the long history of suffering and disaster that we owe to Rome. How do you see this latest example of her rudeness and aggression? Event number one: "snubbing the Volsci". Or perhaps you don't realise that today you were the victims again? That your retreat was seen by hundreds of Romans, and others from round about? That your wives and children were the prize exhibits? Just imagine for a moment what people must be thinking. Perhaps they heard the official announcement, perhaps they saw us leaving Rome or slinking along the road here – either way, in their eyes we are criminals. As far as they can see, we've been expelled because, if we took part in the Games, we'd somehow defile them by our presence. And that's not all. Has it occurred to you that we'd have been killed if we hadn't left so quickly? I say "left"; perhaps "run away" is more like it. Any city where I can't stay for one day without getting murdered, I'd call that city enemy territory. Or don't you agree? This is war! And if I'm right about you, the Romans will be sorry they started it.'

This speech made them all angrier still. When they got back to their towns and villages they spread the word and soon the whole tribe was ready for a fight. They chose two leaders by popular vote, Tullius and Coriolanus. If anything, the Roman exile got the greater support of the two. He soon showed that he deserved it. So much so that the Volsci drew an obvious conclusion: the Roman army was nothing special – Rome owed her successes to her generals. First of all Coriolanus marched to Circeii, threw out the Roman settlers, 'liberated' it and handed it over to the Volsci. He then captured four towns the Romans had only recently taken over, including Corioli; reoccupied Lavinium; marched across country to the Latin Road; captured five more towns. From Pedum, the last of these, he marched as far as the Trenches of Cluilius, about five miles from Rome. From here raiding parties went out to smash up the Roman farms. Coriolanus appointed special officers to make sure the raiders spared any farms belonging to the patricians. Perhaps this was to get his own back on the plebeians, or perhaps he just wanted to stir up class warfare. Anyway, this certainly broke out with a vengeance. The plebeians were militant enough as it was, but the tribunes now began to make complaint after complaint and do all they could to set the plebeians at their masters' throats.

The only thing that kept this hatred and suspicion from getting out of control was the threat from outside. As usual, common danger put political squabbles in the shade. However there was one point on which the two parties stood firmly opposed. The Senate and the consuls were quite sure that war was the only answer. The plebeians refused to consider it. Matters came to a head one day when the consuls, Nautius and Furius, were out reviewing the troops and giving their advice on the defences. To their alarm, a huge, unruly mob advanced on them shouting 'We want peace!' Then they made the consuls call a meeting of the Senate and suggest sending people to Coriolanus to negotiate. The Senate could see the plebeians were on the verge of rebellion, so they agreed.

The peace mission went to Coriolanus and brought back a tough reply:

'Give the Volsci back the territory you've taken, then peace talks can start. But if you think you can hold on to it without a fight, I should warn you: the Romans' insults and the Volsci's generosity are both fresh in my mind. You'll see that exile hasn't crushed me, just made me more determined than ever.'

The Romans sent the same negotiators back to try again. This time Coriolanus refused to let them in the camp. Even the priests, the story goes, dressed in their official robes, went to beg for peace. They too failed to have any effect. At this point the women of Rome came in large numbers to his mother Veturia, and to his wife Volumnia. I cannot say for certain whether this was a scheme they had thought out or whether they were really afraid. But in any case the two women agreed to what the others suggested: namely for Veturia, old as she was, and Volumnia to take Coriolanus' two young sons and go to the camp and see him. If the men were not going to defend Rome with swords, at least the women could try with tears.

They reached the camp. Coriolanus was informed that a large crowd of women had come to see him. His first reaction was to ignore them – hardly surprising, when he had already turned a deaf ear to official negotiators and to priests in their most impressive robes. Then one of his aides noticed Veturia, standing between Volumnia and the two boys and obviously in the greatest distress:

'Unless my eyes deceive me, that is your mother there, with your wife and children.'

Almost in a frenzy, Coriolanus sprang to his feet. He ran to put his arms round his mother, but she turned on him suddenly in a blaze of anger:

'Tell me, before I receive any kisses from you, are you my enemy or my son? Am I in this camp as your prisoner or as your mother? Is this to be the reward of my long life and miserable old age, to see you first an exile and then an enemy? To think that you could plunder this land which bore you and fed you! I can imagine how angry you were as you marched to the Roman border. But when you actually crossed it, didn't your fury subside? When the walls of Rome were in sight, didn't a voice inside you say, "Within those walls are my home and the gods that guard it, my mother, my wife, my children"? If I had never been a mother, Rome would not now be in danger. If I had had no son, I could die free, in a free city. I can sink no further in misery than this, and you can sink no lower in shame. But whatever I suffer, it won't be for long. Think of your wife and children! If Rome falls, what have they to look forward to? An early death or a life of slavery.'

His wife and his two sons flung their arms around him. Meanwhile the other women were all in tears, weeping for themselves and for Rome. Finally Coriolanus gave way. He kissed his family and sent them home. Then he struck camp and took the army out of Roman territory.

There are several versions of the end of this story. One says that the Volsci never forgave his treachery and that their resentment killed him. The oldest version is given by the historian Fabius. He writes that Coriolanus lived to a ripe old age. Or, to be more precise, he quotes one of Coriolanus' favourite sayings at the end of his life:

'Exile is harder to bear when you're old.'

Rome was involved in more fighting during the next thirty years. There was also continuous unrest among the plebeians and finally, in 461, mob rioting. They claimed that too much land was in the hands of just a few landowners; and that it was time some laws were passed to protect the ordinary citizen – as it was, consuls were even worse than kings because there were two of them instead of one. The problems inside Rome were made worse by the sheer size of the population. According to a census held in 464, there were 104,714 citizens, and this did not include their families.

One of the few men to emerge with honour from the political infighting was Lucius Quinctius Cincinnatus. All his money had gone to pay his son Caeso's debts. He lived on a tiny farm outside Rome. But he refused to break the law by standing for consul two years running and reckoned the Senate had brought a lot of the political trouble on itself by being so feeble. In 458 one of the consuls, Minucius, managed to get himself surrounded by an army of the Aequi. Five soldiers got through and brought the news to Rome.

CINCINNATUS

This was the last thing the Romans had expected. From the terror and confusion it caused you would have thought it was the city that was surrounded. The other consul, Nautius, was ordered to present himself but it soon became clear he was not the man for a situation like this. What it needed was a Dictator. Everyone agreed it had to be Lucius Quinctius Cincinnatus.

Now if you are one of those people who are only interested in money, and think that honesty and ability by themselves are worth nothing . . . well, read this story. Lucius Quinctius, Rome's last hope and defence, was at that moment working on his land – a farm of well under three acres, the plot known today as Quinctius' Meadow; it is just opposite the shipyards west of the Tiber. This is where the messengers from the Senate found him, digging maybe, or ploughing – anyway, hard at work in the fields. They exchanged greetings. His visitors then asked him to put on his toga and receive the Senate's instructions; it was a matter of importance, they said, for his own future and Rome's as well. He was very surprised and asked anxiously if everything was all right. Then he told his wife Racilia to run to the cottage and fetch his toga. She did so and when he had wiped off the worst of the dust and sweat, he put it on. At once the messengers congratulated him on his appointment as Dictator. They explained the danger the army was in and asked him to come with them to Rome.

An official ship took them back to the city where a welcoming committee was waiting for him: his three sons and other relatives, friends, and most of the senators. They went with him to his town house, with the lictors leading the way. The rest of the Roman population also turned out in force, but they were not nearly so happy to see this procession. For them, any Dictator was too powerful. And they were afraid Cincinnatus would use his powers all too thoroughly.

That night a watch was set in the city but nothing else was done. Next day Cincinnatus was in the forum before dawn and appointed Lucius Tarquitius as his cavalry commander. Tarquitius was a nobleman, but being poor he had done all his service in the infantry. Even so, he was recognised as the best soldier the Romans had. The two of them appeared at the usual open-air meeting and Cincinnatus gave his orders:

'The law courts will be shut and so will shops all over the city. There's to be no private business of any kind. All men of military age will parade fully equipped in the Campus Martius* before sunset. They will bring with them five days' supply of cooked food and twelve stakes. While they're collecting these and getting their equipment ready,those of you who are too old to join up can help by seeing to their food.'

There was instant activity. In the hunt for stakes they were taken from anywhere they could be found. No one objected. The men duly paraded and Cincinnatus took charge of the legions, Tarquitius of the cavalry. Then they set off on their march in a formation which could be used for fighting if they had to. By midnight they reached Mount Algidus. They realised the Aequi couldn't be far away so they halted and Cincinnatus rode off to have a look around. Even though it was dark, he got some idea of the size and layout of the enemy camp. He came back with orders for his officers:

'Tell the men to dump all their packs in a single pile. They're to keep just their weapons and stakes and then fall back into line.'

They did so, and Cincinnatus stationed them in a huge circle round the enemy camp without having to move anyone out of his marching position. The orders were to wait for a signal and then raise a battle-cry. After that they were to start digging where they stood and sticking in their stakes. The signal duly came and the plan went into action. Shouting broke out all round and the noise carried beyond the Aequi to Minucius' men in the centre of the two circles. The Aequi were terrified, but the consul's army was delighted: those were Romans shouting – help had arrived! Without waiting for orders, the sentries of the surrounded Roman army moved into the attack. In fact Minucius realised that immediate action was vital:

48

'That shouting must mean they haven't only got into position, they're actually on the move, probably up to the Aequi's outer defences by now. Arm yourselves and follow me!'

> In the battle that followed, the Aequi found two Roman armies, front and back, too much for them. Cincinnatus spared their lives, but made them go under the yoke to show that they surrendered absolutely.

He then let them go, with the minimum of clothing. So, when the Romans took over the Aequian camp, there was plenty of everything. Cincinnatus turned it all over to his own men. Minucius and his army had to make do with some pieces of strong criticism:

'You needn't expect any enemy property to come your way', said Cincinnatus, 'considering you were nearly enemy property yourselves. As for you, Minucius, until you show signs of behaving like a consul you will remain as my second-in-command.'

Minucius promptly resigned his consulship and stayed with the army as ordered. His men were quite happy to serve under a man of Cincinnatus' qualities. Any shame they felt was outweighed by gratitude. To prove this, they gave him a solid gold wreath weighing a pound and, when he finally left them, hailed him as their saviour.

In Rome the city prefect called a special meeting of the Senate and they invited Cincinnatus to bring his army inside the city for an official triumph. In front of the Dictator's chariot came the enemy leaders and the Roman standards; behind came the victorious army carrying the spoils of war. They say that every house had a table outside it piled with food, for the chanting, joking crowd that joined the procession. It was like one enormous party.

The only thing that stopped Cincinnatus resigning his dictatorship was a trial that was coming up. A man called Marcus Volscius was accused of giving false evidence against one of Cincinnatus' sons. The tribunes were too frightened of Cincinnatus to interfere, so Volscius was found guilty and exiled. Then Cincinnatus did resign. He had taken on the job for six months. He left it after just fifteen days.

> Livy does not say how old Cincinnatus was at this time. Probably in his fifties because his son Caeso was already old enough to be a powerful man in Rome. Nearly twenty years later, in 439, Cincinnatus was again appointed Dictator to settle a quarrel inside the city. Somewhere around this time (some say 451,

others 449) the Romans agreed on twelve basic laws that would apply to everybody. These are known as the Twelve Tables. Even so, squabbles between patricians and plebeians continued.

Ever since it was founded, Rome had had trouble with the Etruscan city of Veii, ten miles (16 km) away (see map, p. 6). Veii was older than Rome and extremely rich. It seems likely that the quarrels were over money since both cities were involved in trade. From about 437 Rome mounted a series of campaigns against Veii, but it took them nearly fifty years before they captured it. They did so around 394, led by Marcus Furius Camillus. Two years later Camillus set out to capture Falerii, the capital of the Falisci (see map, p. 6) which had been on Veii's side.

CAMILLUS AND THE SCHOOLTEACHER

Next the Romans surrounded the town of Falerii and hemmed it in all round with a wall of earth. From time to time the Faliscans would rush out and there would be a brief skirmish. But on both sides hopes of victory were slim. For one thing the Faliscans had laid in a lot of corn and other supplies before the siege started. They were in fact better off in this respect than the Romans. So it looked as though the Romans were in for a long, boring siege, as at Veii. Then Camillus had a piece of luck. He was given a chance to show his sense of fair play and, what is more, bring the campaign to a quick end.

In Falerii schoolteachers normally acted as both teachers and supervisors. As in Greece today, several boys were often under the control of one man. The sons of the most important citizens were naturally taught by the man everybody reckoned to be the best qualified for the job. Before the siege this man had got into the habit of taking his boys out in front of the city walls for their games and exercises. When the campaign began he went on doing so, sometimes just outside, sometimes quite a long way away, depending on the game they were playing or the discussion they were having.

One day they went further than usual. The schoolteacher seized his chance and led them past the Roman guards, into the camp and right up to Camillus in his headquarters. He then proved he really was a traitor by saying, 'I hereby deliver the sons of the leading citizens into your power – Falerii is yours.' Camillus replied, 'I see from the present you bring that treachery is your trade. Well, it has never been the Romans' trade, nor is it mine. I know our two peoples are not joined by any formal treaty. But we are still joined for ever by the fact that we are human beings. War, like peace, has its rules, and we Romans have learnt to practise honesty as well as courage. We are not here to fight children – boys as young as this are never harmed, even when a city is captured. No, we have come to fight fighting men – the men who attacked the Roman camp at Veii without the slightest provocation. You have done your best to defeat them by this novel form of treachery. I shall defeat them the Roman way, as I did at Veii, with courage, energy and military skill.' Camillus had the man stripped and his hands tied behind him. Then he gave him to the boys to take back to Falerii. He gave them sticks too, so they could thrash the traitor all the way home.

In Falerii a huge crowd gathered to watch the scene and shortly afterwards the assembly met to discuss the whole extraordinary business. Until this meeting the citizens had been seething with hatred for Rome, almost demanding death before surrender; now there was a total change of heart – they were clamouring for peace with one voice. Privately in the marketplace and publicly in the assembly, everyone was talking about the honesty of the Romans and their leader. After a unanimous vote representatives were sent to Camillus in his camp. With his permission they then went on to the Senate in Rome to surrender Falerii.

They were taken to the senate-house and are said to have spoken as follows: 'Senators of Rome, you and Camillus are victorious and no one, either god or man, could grudge you this victory. We surrender to you in the belief that we shall have a better life under your government than under our own laws. No victor could ask for a finer compliment than that. This war has provided two splendid lessons for mankind: you have put honour in war before instant victory; and we have been inspired by this to surrender of our own free will. We are in your power. Take our weapons, take our hostages: the city gates lie open before you. You may rely on our loyalty, as we shall on your honest government.'

Camillus was given a vote of thanks by both sides. The Faliscans on the other hand were given the job of paying Rome's army for that year, so the Romans would not have to contribute to the war fund. A peace treaty was agreed and the Roman troops came home.

3　The invasion of the Gauls

Rome had won a leading position in Central Italy in wars fought against other Italian tribes, when the Romans knew roughly what sort of tactics to expect. They also knew what sort of men their opponents were and what sort of treatment they would get if they were captured. The Gauls provided their first struggle with the unknown. They were a tribe forming part of a much larger population group, known as the Celts. The Celts had a common language and artistic tradition: they lived north of the Mediterranean, in an area stretching from Spain, through France, and along the Danube to the Black Sea. Apparently there was a story that these invaders were attracted to Italy by the wine! But whatever the reason, Livy, as so often, suggests that Fate was really behind it all:

THE GAULS ON THE WARPATH: 391 – 390 B.C.

One day a plebeian called Marcus Caedicius came to the tribunes with a strange story:

'One night', he said, 'I was walking along the New Street. Suddenly, in the silence, an enormous voice came booming out: "Go and tell your rulers that the Gauls are coming!" '

Now Caedicius was nobody of any importance and, as you might expect, the tribunes just laughed. The Gauls lived a long way north and so were an almost unknown factor. But even if the Romans chose to ignore this warning from heaven, the wheels of Fate were beginning to turn. In fact the Romans went further than simply ignoring it: they expelled from Rome the one man they could rely on, Marcus Furius Camillus.

One of the tribunes of the people, called Lucius Apuleius, charged him with corruption over the handling of the plunder from Veii. Moreover, he did this just after Camillus had lost his young son. Camillus held a meeting at his house for all his local friends and dependants (altogether a sizeable number of the plebeians) and asked what they felt about the charge against him. They replied:

'If you're fined, we'll pay the fine, no matter how big it is. But we can't pretend you're innocent.'

So he went into exile. But before he did so he prayed to the gods:

'If I'm innocent, and this charge is false, may Rome pay for her ingratitude, and soon! May she grovel to have me back again!'

In his absence Camillus was fined 15,000 *asses*.* He, if anyone, might have prevented Rome being captured. But now that he was gone, disaster began to move in upon the city. A message was brought to Rome from the people of Clusium. Would the Romans help them to fight off the Gauls?

The men of Clusium were seriously alarmed, facing as they did a strange enemy, in their thousands, looking like nothing they had ever seen before. Even their weapons were peculiar. Rumour had it that they had inflicted defeat after defeat on the Etruscans on both sides of the river Po. Clusium had no official ties with Rome and they had never been particularly friendly with each other. The most Clusium could claim was that she had not supported Veii against Rome even though Clusium and Veii had tribal links. But now she was asking the Roman Senate for help.

The Senate refused to send an army. Instead they in turn sent negotiators to the Gauls. The three sons of Marcus Fabius Ambustus were chosen to deliver the following message on behalf of the Roman people:

'Clusium is an ally and friend of Rome. They have never caused you any trouble or given you any reason to attack them and, if it comes to the point, we shall defend the town by force. But we would much rather avoid bloodshed altogether if we can and make your acquaintance as friends.'

The message itself was tactfully phrased. But the three brothers delivered it in a very rude and violent manner. You might say they behaved more like Gauls than Romans. The Gauls replied:

'We have never heard of Rome before. But we're quite willing to believe it is a powerful city, otherwise Clusium wouldn't have asked for your help in her present troubles. You say you would rather help your friends by talking than by fighting? Well, we're not ones to despise the value of peace. But we need land. Now, Clusium has more than she can cope with. If she gives us some of it, the matter's settled. But if not, then peace is out of the question. And we'd like an answer while you Romans are still here. Then, if the answer is "No", you can see us in action; and go home afterwards and tell them all that the Gauls are the best soldiers on earth.'

'This is your idea of justice, is it', replied the Romans, 'saying to people with land, "Hand over or else!"'? What are you doing in Etruria anyway?'

'Force is our justice' came the retort, 'and force is the only thing that counts.'

Both sides, Gauls and Etruscans, were now furiously angry. The negotiations broke up and a pitched battle ensued. Once more Fate moved against Rome: the three Roman negotiators joined in the fight, something that was universally agreed to be a breach of faith. There was no hiding the fact either. The three of them outshone all the Etruscans in skill and daring. But Quintus Fabius went out of his way to draw attention to himself. He rode out of the cavalry formation and towards the Gallic general, who was making straight for the Etruscan standards.* Then he ran him through with his spear and killed him. As he began to strip the body, the Gauls recognised him. Word went through the whole army that this was one of the Roman negotiators. At once the quarrel with Clusium was forgotten. The Gauls pulled out of the battle, their thoughts turned against Rome.

Some of the Gauls were all for marching on Rome straight away. But in the end they followed their elders' advice and sent a mission to complain about what had happened. They also insisted on the three Fabii being handed over as criminals. These points were duly made. The Roman Senate could not approve of the brothers' behaviour, in fact they thought what the Gauls were asking was perfectly reasonable. But there was a difference between knowing what was right and doing it. After all, these three men were noblemen like themselves. They were afraid too that they would get the blame if it came to a fight with the Gauls, and the Romans lost. So they asked the people to deal with the Gauls' request. This was where the power of snobbery and wealth made itself felt. The business started with discussions about how the three men were to be punished; it ended with them being appointed military tribunes for the following year, with the authority of consuls added. Understandably the Gauls were furious. Before they left for home, they made it quite clear that the next step was war.

Once Fate is in motion there is no stopping her advance. She has the power of blinding men to the truth. Just so in this case . . . In previous years, when fighting Fidenae or Veii or some other nearby town, Rome had often gone to the extreme of appointing a Dictator. Now they faced the most terrible danger and an unfamiliar enemy – an enemy they had barely heard of, marching towards them from the shores of the Atlantic Ocean. And now they chose to keep the command structure just as it was. The tribunes were in charge. Their hot-headed behaviour had caused the war, but they showed no particular energy in raising an army, no more than for any other regular campaign. They even claimed the situation was not all that serious.

Meanwhile the Gauls wasted no time. They were angry at the Romans for promoting common criminals to be their leaders, and for ignoring their own request so completely. And when a Gaul is angry there is no holding him. With banners flying they were marching south as fast as they could. As they roared past, citizens armed themselves in terror and farmers came running inside the walls for protection. But this immense, chaotic mass of men and horses did not stop to attack them. As they passed, the cry could be heard: 'To Rome.'

Rumour soon reached the Romans of what was happening, then came official reports from Clusium and elsewhere. Even so the sheer speed of the advance was daunting. The Romans got some sort of army together as quickly as they could but had gone a mere eleven miles before they met their enemy, at a place where the river Allia runs through a gorge on its way down the mountainside and then joins the Tiber just south of the road. To the front, to left and right, the whole area was swarming with Gauls. And, as they are noisy and riotous by nature, the air was thick with ferocious screams and yells.

The Roman leaders took no precautions on their troops' behalf; they did not choose a place for a camp, they had no defensive mound built to shelter a retreat. They even forgot the gods. There was no ritual observation of birds, no animals were sacrificed or inspected. As they were frightened of being out-flanked by the enemy's enormous numbers they stretched their battle-line over a wide front. This left the centre perilously thin, and even then the Gauls overlapped them on both flanks. A little to the right there was a small patch of high ground. Here the Romans put their reserves – a fact which led to the initial breaking of the Romans' spirit but also gave them some hope of escaping. Brennus, the Gallic chieftain, looking at the Romans' meagre forces, was sure they must be planning a trap. The reserves on the hill, he reckoned, would wait until he attacked the Romans head-on, and then come swooping down on his flank and rear. So he made them his first target. Once they had been dislodged, he was certain that on the flat his larger numbers could settle the matter without much trouble.

The Gauls were lucky, but at least there was some plan behind their movements. On the Roman side there was absolutely no sign of the traditional spirit or discipline at any level. They were numb with panic. All they could think about was running away. Most of them even ignored the open road to Rome and their own families. Instead they tried to cross the Tiber and escape to Veii, their old enemy. For a few moments the reserves, in their stronger position, held firm. The rest of the army heard shouting from the flanks and rear, and that was enough. They hardly waited to see their unknown enemy, let alone fight or return their challenge. They saved their skins and ran. None of them was killed fighting. They were cut down from behind as they tried to push their way through their comrades.

The whole of the left flank threw away their swords and headed for the Tiber. The near bank became the scene of the most terrible bloodshed. Some of them, unable to swim or exhausted by the weight of their equipment, were drowned in the swirling waters. But most of them got to Veii without a scratch. Not one soldier left Veii for Rome, to help defend her or even to bring news of their defeat. The right flank had been stationed some way from the Tiber, near the high ground. They fled to Rome in a body and took refuge in the citadel. They did not even bother to shut the outer gates.

The speed of it all left the Gauls quite stunned. They stood around blankly, as though wondering what on earth had happened. Was there still some trap waiting for them? Eventually they set to work stripping the fallen bodies and making a pile of the weapons, as usual. Still the Romans did not reappear. So at last they began to march and just before sunset reached the walls of Rome. They sent some cavalry ahead to have a look round; the gates were not closed, there were no sentries guarding them, there were no soldiers on the walls. For a second time that day, they were stunned. They were also nervous of entering an unknown city in the dark. So they sent another party out to investigate the walls and the rest of the gates, and to try and find out what plans, if any, the Romans had for coping with their desperate situation. Then they set up camp between the city and the river Anio.

THE GAULS IN ROME

Most of the Roman army had gone westwards to Veii rather than south to Rome. As a result everyone thought that the ones who *had* returned to Rome were the only survivors. Almost the whole city resounded with the noise of mourning, equally loud for those who were dead and for those who were still alive. But the sorrows of private citizens soon gave way to more general alarm, when the news broke that the Gauls had arrived. Indeed before long the Romans could see groups of them roaming about outside the walls, and hear their howls and raucous chanting.

With every minute that passed between then and the following morning the Romans waited for the attack to be launched: when the Gauls first arrived, they asked, 'Why else are they here? If they weren't going to attack Rome they'd have stayed up by the Allia'; then as it got near dusk, 'Not much daylight left now: they're bound to attack before it gets dark'; then as the sun went down, 'They're playing on our fear, leaving the attack till night-time.' The whole city was weak with terror by the time dawn came and with it the Gauls. Fear had turned into fact.

Even so this period of night and day found a very different Rome from the one whose army had made such a cowardly escape on the Allia. Clearly there was no question of defending the whole city with such a small handful of men. Instead it was decided to send all the able-bodied men and senators, with the women and children, up to the fortress on the Capitol hill. As long as they were supplied with weapons and food, they could hold out here, defending their gods and Rome's reputation. The priest and priestesses of Vesta* were to take the sacred vessels far away from the flames and bloodshed and go on with their rituals as long as there was anyone left to conduct them. So Rome concentrated on the three essentials: the Capitol, the home of the gods; the Senate, the real government; and her army. If she could save these three from the destruction that was about to come upon her, then it was a small sacrifice to leave the old men down in the city. They did not have long to live in any case. To get the plebeians to accept this decision without too much protest, the older members of the Senate, once Rome's leaders in peace and war, publicly agreed to join them: 'We shall die side by side with you. These bodies of ours can no longer fight to defend our city. They shall not eat the food of those who can.'

This was the sort of comfort the old men gave themselves in the face of death. Then they turned to encouraging the young men as they saw them on their way to the Capitol. For three hundred and sixty years Rome had never lost a war. Now her future, if any, lay in the courage and resilience of this small band. The moment came for the two groups to part: one bearing Rome's hope and strength, one choosing to die as the city fell. It was a melancholy scene, made worse by the women running about and crying hysterically. Should they go with their husbands? Or with their sons? They pleaded with their menfolk to make this terrible decision for them. In the end, most of them went with their sons up to the Capitol. Obviously, from the military point of view, the fewer non-combatants on the hill the better. So no one actually encouraged them. At the same time no one had the heart to try and stop them. But the summit of the Capitol is very small in area. Space and food were both severely limited. So another large crowd, mostly of plebeians, began to stream out of Rome, heading for the Janiculum. From here some set out to wander the countryside, others went to towns nearby. They had no leaders, no agreed plans. For them, Rome was a thing of the past. Each man now had to make his own future.

Meanwhile the priest of Quirinus* and the Vestal Virgins were not thinking about themselves but about the sacred objects in their care. Because they could not carry everything they had to decide what to take, what to leave behind and where to leave it safely. In the end they agreed to hide the objects in casks and bury them in the shrine next to the priest's house (the place, in fact, where spitting is still considered blasphemous). They took what they could carry and began to walk along the road that leads over the pontoon bridge to the Janiculum. As they were toiling up the slope a plebeian called Lucius Albinius spotted them. He too was leaving Rome like the rest of the civilian population, with his wife and children in a horse and cart. Even at this desperate moment Albinius was alive to his religious duty. It was sacrilege, he thought, for the priestesses of Vesta and the sacred vessels of Rome to be going on foot while he and his family were riding in a cart for all to see. He told them to get down and took the Vestal Virgins and their holy objects to their journey's end at Caere.

At Rome, meanwhile, preparations for defending the Capitol were more or less complete. The old men were back in their homes, waiting for the Gauls and certain death. Some of them had in the past presided over the public Games. Now they waited to die wearing their most splendid ceremonial robes, to remind them of a time when they had been powerful and respected men in Rome. There they sat, in their central courtyards, on chairs inlaid with ivory. We are told also that Marcus Folius, the chief priest, led them in chanting a solemn vow, sacrificing themselves for Rome and her people.

The Gauls entered the city next day. They showed no signs of anger or ferocity. They had had the whole night to cool down from the heat of battle, not that they had been in danger of defeat for a moment. And now they were taking Rome without a hand raised against them. The Colline Gate was open and as they made for the forum they looked about them at the holy temples – and at the Capitol, from which came the only signs of Roman resistance. They posted a small garrison in case the Romans came charging down on them as they wandered round the city. Then it was every man for himself. There was no one in the streets to stop them, and looting began in the first houses they came to. Some headed straight for the suburbs, thinking the houses there would be stuffed with untouched treasure. But everything there was so quiet . . . They were terrified the Romans had some trap laid to catch small groups separated from the main body. Keeping close together they came back to the forum and the area round it.

The plebeians' houses were shut and bolted, and the Gauls had no hesitation in breaking down the doors. The nobles' houses were open, but here the Gauls were reluctant to enter. As they looked through the doorways at the old men sitting in their courtyards, they felt a sort of religious fear come over them. The robes and insignia were more majestic than anything the Gauls had ever seen on a human being; the dignity in those calm, stern faces made them seem like gods. For a time they stood staring at these statue-like figures. Then one of them went up to a senator called Marcus Papirius and began to stroke his beard, a long one as the fashion was in those days. Papirius reacted by beating him furiously over the head with his ivory staff. That was the start of the massacre. The other senators were killed where they sat. When the Gauls had finished with them they began to slaughter the rest wholesale, while all around houses were wrecked and set on fire.

Even so, there was no question of the fire sweeping through everything that first day, as often happens in captured cities. Perhaps there were some Gauls opposed to destroying Rome completely. Or perhaps the Gallic leaders were deliberately controlling the amount of havoc their men caused: enough damage to the Romans' homes and property to frighten them and make them think about surrender, but at the same time enough left untouched for the invaders to bargain with.

From the Capitol the Romans looked down on their city swarming with hostile foreigners. Wherever they looked, some new disaster struck. They were seized with a sort of paralysis: their minds, even their eyes and ears, refused to take in what was happening. But, terrified as they were, they could not drag themselves away from the scene, from the enemy war-cries, the howling of women and children, the roar of the flames and the crash of falling buildings. It was as if Fortune had given them grandstand seats for a show called 'The Death of Rome'. Their own bodies were all they had left. To be besieged at all is a terrible experience. But it was worse still for the Romans, being besieged *outside* their city and seeing everything they owned in enemy hands.

That night brought no comfort for their troubles. The looting went on next day and every moment provided some new horror. But in spite of their desperate situation, their morale never collapsed. Even if the whole city was smashed and burnt, however cramped and short of food they might be, they were still determined to hold on to the Capitol as the last home of freedom. Every day it was the same pattern of destruction. Before long they found themselves getting used to it; they simply did not care any more about what they had lost. Instead they started thinking about their only hope for the future – their shields and swords.

For some days the Gauls employed their energy attacking the city's buildings. But all their burning and pillaging only reduced Rome to a nucleus of armed soldiers. In spite of all they had been through, the Romans obviously had no intention of surrendering. The Gauls would have to use force. So they decided to risk a direct attack on the Capitol. At dawn next day the order went round and the whole Gallic army assembled in the forum. The war-cry was heard; shields were locked above their heads. The ascent began.

The Romans reacted cautiously but confidently. All paths up to the summit were guarded and the Romans' best troops were stationed in line with the attack. They let the Gauls come some way up the slope, believing that 'the higher they climb, the harder they fall'. About half way up the Gauls paused. At this moment the Romans came hurtling down with all the force of the slope behind them and routed the Gauls with heavy losses. After this the Gauls dropped the idea of any sort of direct attack. If force could not succeed, then they would have to embark on a blockade. This was something they had not foreseen. All the grain inside the city had gone up in the blaze, while the Romans had hurriedly gathered what was standing in the fields just during the last few days and sent it off to Veii. So the Gauls had to split their army. One part went off plundering the countryside round about, to feed the other part which now settled down to blockade the Capitol.

CAMILLUS AGAIN

Strangely enough, the Gauls had to leave Rome to get their first real taste of Roman courage. Rome's destiny led the marauders to Ardea, where Camillus was living in exile. He was far more depressed about Rome's situation than about his own. As he grew older, he had hard words for gods and men alike, and was given to indignant outbursts: 'Where are the soldiers I led into Veii and Falerii? They relied on courage not luck.' Then one day he heard the news that an army of Gauls was on the way to Ardea; and that the townsmen were anxiously discussing what to do. So far Camillus had never taken part in any of their meetings. But now some god must have inspired him. He came bursting into the council chamber:

'Gentlemen, you have been my friends for many years, and more recently my fellow citizens. You took me in when luck was against me. So please don't think, from the way I've rushed in here, that I've forgotten my place in the community. But this danger threatens us all. In times like this we must pool our ideas. If ever there was a time for me to say "thank you" for all your kindness, this is it. A campaign gives me the perfect opportunity to be of service. Warfare was the area in which I won my reputation in Rome, and in warfare I was never beaten. It was only when peace came that the Romans turned ungrateful and exiled me. This, gentlemen, is your chance to pay Rome back for all the help she has given you over the years – I needn't bore you with the details, you know what I mean. It's also your chance to win fame and glory from this common enemy.

What then of this disorganised mass heading towards us? They are large men, certainly, and they have a sort of courage. But they're not steady. So whenever it comes to a battle, they look much tougher and more terrifying than they really are. Take this last victory over the Romans. They walk into an open city, and find they can't dislodge a tiny handful of men on the Capitol. They get bored with a blockade and now they're roaming aimlessly all over the countryside. They stuff themselves full of food and wine and then at the end of the day they never think of building defences or posting sentries; they just sprawl along the river banks. They're no better than wild animals. And now that things have gone so much their way, they're even more careless than usual. You do want to save your city? And prevent this whole area becoming another bit of Gaul? Very well then – as soon as it's dark, arm yourselves, every man of you, and follow me. It won't be a battle, it'll be a massacre. I'll hand them to you sleeping like logs – and you can butcher them like cattle. And if I fail, then you have my permission to treat me as the Romans did.'

Not all of those present were on friendly terms with Camillus, but everyone agreed that he was the finest general of his time. The meeting broke up and they went off to eat and get ready. Then came the eagerly awaited signal. Through the dark, silent streets they came to the city gates where Camillus was waiting. A short march out of the city brought them, as he had promised, to the Gallic camp. With yells of triumph they attacked. There was no resistance to the wholesale slaughter that followed. The Gauls were killed before they could arm themselves or even wake up properly. Those on the outskirts of the army, even if they had time to wake up, still did not know what had hit them or where it was coming from. As a result, some of them ran in a panic straight into the arms of their attackers. Most of them, however, managed to reach the neighbourhood of Antium. Here they wandered about for a time till the men of the town came out and rounded them up.

At Rome, meanwhile, the blockade of the Capitol was a slow and unexciting business. The Gauls' only concern was to stop anybody slipping through their net. The monotony was shattered by a young Roman soldier, whose exploit left both sides equally in astonished admiration. Every year the Quirinal hill was the scene of a sacrifice, conducted by the family of the Fabii. On the appointed day Gaius Fabius Dorsuo began to make his way down the Capitol hill, dressed in his ceremonial toga and carrying the sacred vessels. He walked right through the enemy lines, ignoring shouts and threats, and reached the Quirinal hill. He carried out the complete ceremony, and then returned the way he had come, with not a sign of alarm or haste. As he had risked his life to do his duty to the gods, no doubt he relied on them to protect him. He got back to his friends on the Capitol, leaving the Gauls open-mouthed at his extraordinary courage. Or perhaps they respected his religious principles – they do take religion very seriously.

Meanwhile the situation in Veii was improving daily. Morale and numbers were both rising. Some of the arrivals were Romans who had survived the battle on the Allia or had been at large since the Gauls entered Rome, but there were also numerous volunteers from all over Latium who were keen to be in at the kill and take the pickings. The time had come to march on Rome and expel the Gauls.

But this body of men, strong as it was, still had no head. The name 'Veii' at once suggested 'Camillus', and many of these soldiers had won battles under his command. Everyone agreed that he should be summoned from Ardea. But even in this desperate situation they took care to observe the proper formalities: before sending for Camillus, they would have to consult the Senate in Rome.

Getting through the enemy lines was now a highly dangerous operation. An energetic young man called Pontius Cominus offered to try and reach Rome by floating down the Tiber on a cork raft. He landed and took a short cut to the Capitol up a face of rock so steep that the Gauls had not bothered to guard it. He was taken to the magistrates and delivered the army's request. The Senate duly decided and pronounced: 'By order of the people and the lawfully appointed assembly, Camillus is hereby recalled from exile, and is to be named Dictator forthwith, that the army may have the general they desire.' Cominus took this message back to Veii and further messengers then went to fetch Camillus from Ardea.

ALARMS AND CONCLUSION

During all this the Capitol went through a severe crisis. It seems the Gauls may have spotted the tracks left by Cominus, or perhaps they just happened to notice that by the shrine of Carmenta there was a path, rocky but quite climbable. Anyway, they waited for a night that was not too bright and not too dark and sent an unarmed man ahead to test the route. Then they started to scramble up. Where it was particularly steep they had to hand their weapons up first, and altogether there was a lot of pushing and pulling to get over the various obstacles. But they reached the top with hardly a sound. The Roman sentries noticed nothing. Even the dogs went on sleeping – and in the night dogs will bark at anything. Only the geese heard them. They were sacred to Juno and, although food was very short, no one had been willing to commit sacrilege. Without them, Rome would have fallen. The noise of their honking and flapping woke up Marcus Manlius. He had been one of the consuls three years before and was a first-class soldier. Grabbing his sword and shield, he shouted to his friends to arm themselves. Even as they were recovering from the shock, the first Gaul was up and into the citadel. Manlius rushed at him and with the boss of his shield sent him spinning to the foot of the cliff. As he fell he scattered those round him. Many of the rest dropped their weapons in terror and Manlius despatched them as they clung to the rocks. Then his comrades joined him and started hurling javelins and stones. The whole of the surprise force was dislodged and fell headlong to their deaths.

The commotion died down. Nothing else happened that night but the thought of how close they had come to disaster made peaceful slumber rather difficult for the Romans. At dawn the trumpet sounded for a general parade before the tribunes. Now was the time for distributing rewards, and punishments. First the tribunes congratulated Manlius on his brave conduct. Then they and the whole army gave him presents: each man came to Manlius' house on the Capitol bringing half a pound of flour and a quarter of a pint of wine. This may not seem very much, but to do Manlius this honour, each man was depriving himself of food and drink that he really needed; by now the food shortage was serious, so this gesture shows very clearly how grateful they were. Then it was the turn of the guards who had allowed the Gauls to slip through. Quintus Sulpicius, the military tribune,* made it clear he intended to punish them all in the regulation manner. At this there were cries of protest from the whole army: only one of the guards was to blame. Sulpicius gave in, and with general approval the guilty man was punished – flung down from the top of the cliff. The guards on both sides now began to operate rather more efficiently. The Gauls were disturbed by rumours that messengers were travelling between Veii and Rome. The Romans could hardly forget the danger they had been in that night.

But whatever the military problems, both sides suffered even more from hunger. On top of this the Gauls were attacked by fever. Their camp was in an enclosed space and the air was full of hot fumes from the burning city, and, whenever there was a wind, of dust and ashes too. Being used to a cold, damp climate, they found this suffocating atmosphere unbearable. Disease spread among them like cattle and they began to die. They were too weak to bury their dead singly. Instead they threw the bodies into a heap and set fire to them.

At this point a truce was made and official permission given for the two armies to talk to each other. The Gauls kept up a steady run of remarks like 'What's it like to starve, then?' and 'You can't last out much longer, can you?' Apparently the Romans replied by a heavy bombardment with bits of bread. But in fact they were on the edge of starvation and surrender had to come.

All this time Camillus was collecting an army in Ardea. He had told his cavalry commander, Valerius, to bring men from Veii and was now training the assembled troops in the hope of giving the Gauls some serious opposition.

The Romans on the Capitol were exhausted by the strain of the continual watching and waiting. They had coped with every kind of difficulty, but hunger could not be conquered by will-power. Day after day they scanned the horizon for signs of Camillus and his army. At last hope, as well as food, began to fail. When they went on guard, they found they were almost too weak to lift their armour. Surrender or some sort of agreement was the only way out – the Gauls had made it clear enough that they were prepared to abandon the siege for a fairly reasonable sum of money. The Senate met and gave the military tribunes the authority to make peace. So Quintus Sulpicius and Brennus, the Gallic chieftain, duly met and the cost of peace was agreed at one thousand pounds' weight of gold – the price of a city that would one day rule the world. Such a bargain was disgraceful enough, but that was not the end of the matter: the weights which the Gauls had provided were too heavy. Sulpicius complained. Brennus replied by contemptuously throwing his sword as well on to the scales. As he did so, he uttered words well calculated to wound Rome's pride: '*vae victis*' – 'winner takes all'.

But Rome's freedom was not to be bought with gold. Both mortals and immortals saw to that. Thanks to all the delays and arguments, Camillus arrived before this shameful bargain could be agreed. He gave the Gauls his orders:

'That gold goes back where it came from, and as for you, you may leave.'

The Gauls refused, saying the gold had been promised to them.

'You can forget about promises', replied Camillus. 'The deal was made after I was appointed Dictator, by a junior magistrate, without my permission. I suggest you prepare for battle.' He then turned to his own men:

'All packs go in a pile here. You'll need your swords. Win back your city with iron, not gold. Everything that has to be defended or won or avenged is before your eyes: temples, wives, children, and your country's soil bearing the scars of war.'

Every Roman took up his fighting position. The ground was uneven and broken up by the ruins of the city, but Camillus used it as well as he could to give his men an advantage. The Gauls were stunned by the suddenness of it all. They grabbed their weapons and charged wildly, without pausing for thought. Luck was now on the other side. It was the battle of the Allia once again, but this time it was the Gauls who did the running. There was a second, more traditional kind of set battle eight miles out on the road to Gabii, where the Gauls rallied after the initial panic. But again Camillus' leadership was too much for them. The slaughter was complete. The Gauls' camp was taken and not one of them survived even to bring news of the defeat. Rome was saved, and Camillus returned to the city in triumph. The soldiers celebrated with the usual collection of rude jokes, mixed with sincere praise for their leader: a Romulus, the Father of his Country, a second Founder of Rome.

4   Recovery

Though Rome was finally rid of the Gauls, she had to fight for
supremacy over her Italian neighbours all over again. Great
men were needed and soon emerged – but they were not all
blameless heroes . . .

MANLIUS THE TROUBLEMAKER

Rome was now threatened by a serious foreign war and by an
even more serious situation at home. The war involved the Volsci,
together with the Latini and Hernici. On the home front the
trouble came from a most unexpected quarter, a man of good
family and the highest reputation; none other than Marcus Manlius Capitolinus. Manlius looked down on all the other nobles except Camillus, of whom he was jealous. Camillus' reputation and
character were second to none, and Manlius took it hard:

'Why' he grumbled, 'should Camillus be the only great name in
politics and war? He treats his colleagues like servants. But if you
really look at the facts, Camillus couldn't have begun to save
Rome if I hadn't saved the Capitol first. What's more, he beat the
Gauls with their hands full of gold and their minds full of peace;
when I beat them they were carrying swords and on the brink of
capturing the Capitol. Part of his fame too should go to the
soldiers with him, while everyone knows my victory was mine
alone.'

His head was swollen with ideas like these. He was in any case a
hasty and undisciplined sort of person. So when it became clear to
him that the Senate was ignoring his outstanding qualities he
joined the leaders of the plebeians – the first senator ever to go
over to the other side. The Senate now could do nothing right, the
plebeians nothing wrong. Popularity was more valuable than
common-sense and, as long as he was famous, virtue was
irrelevant.

Whenever the tribunes of the people had wanted to cause
trouble in the past, the question of land ownership had always
been a useful weapon. Manlius went further still and brought up

the matter of debt. As he reasoned:

'It's a terrible thing to be in debt. It's not just the lack of money and the disgrace, it's the free man's fear of being thrown into prison and tied up.'

And in fact debt was a major question at this time because of the amount of private building going on, always a big drain on resources, even for the rich. So the Senate decided to set up a higher authority. The war with the Volsci was serious enough to provide an excuse, especially as the Latini and Hernici had joined them. But in appointing a Dictator the Senate was really more worried about Manlius' revolutionary activities. Their choice was Aulus Cornelius Cossus, who in turn chose Titus Quinctius Capitolinus as his cavalry commander.

The campaign was swift and successful. The Dictator kept his army in camp, confident that the Roman Senate would want to take further action against the tribes who had been involved. But the Senate called him home. The trouble in the city was growing and Manlius' reputation meant that things had to be watched even more carefully than usual. He had gone beyond the talking stage and moved into action. His behaviour might look democratic on the surface, but if you knew what lay behind it you could see he was bent on revolution.

Manlius seizes his chance

A centurion* had been condemned for not paying his debts, a man well known in Rome as a brave soldier. As he was being led away, Manlius spotted him. Surrounded by his gang of supporters he pushed his way through the forum and grabbed hold of the man. A long speech followed about the high and mighty Senate, the cruel money-lenders, the poor suffering man-in-the-street and the character and misfortunes of this man in particular; ending with 'It was a waste of effort, I see, saving the Capitol with this right arm. Now I have to look on while a fellow citizen, a fellow soldier of mine, is led away to slavery and a life in chains. The Gauls might just as well have won.'

With these words he paid off the centurion's debt in front of everybody and went through the usual ceremony to show the man was free. The centurion called on heaven and earth to bless Marcus Manlius, his saviour and the father of the Roman people. A riotous crowd immediately gathered round the soldier. He stirred them up still further by showing off the wounds he had received at Veii and from the Gauls and other recent enemies.

'First I was fighting in the army' he explained, 'then I tried to rebuild my house which had been destroyed. During all this the interest on my loan went up and up; I paid off the original sum many times over but I still couldn't get clear. It's only thanks to Marcus Manlius that I'm free to see the sunshine and your faces here in the forum. Manlius has been like a father to me. My remaining strength, my blood, my life are his to command; whatever ties in the past have bound me to Rome and my family, now bind me to this one man.'

His words had a dramatic effect on the crowd, to the extent that 'this one man' could now do what he liked with them. Manlius proceeded to add fuel to the flames. He had a farm near Veii, his most valuable piece of property, and he put it up for auction. 'Fellow citizens', he declared, 'while I have any means at my disposal, no man among you shall be condemned for debt and turned into a slave.' This was the final turn of the screw. He was their champion in the fight for freedom and, right or wrong, they would follow him to the end.

Trouble over gold

His next move was to deliver a number of set speeches in his own house, attacking the Senate. The difference between 'truth' and 'lies' seems not to have bothered him; over the question of the gold, for instance, which had been captured from the Gauls:

'The senators have taken this gold and stowed it away in their vaults. Controlling state land is not enough for them. They have to embezzle public money as well. And this money from the Gauls, if it could find its way to the state treasury, would be enough to release every one of you from debt.'

Dazzled by this prospect, the plebeians came to regard the senators as no better than criminals. 'When Rome's got to be bought back from the Gauls, we all pay for it', they grumbled, 'but as soon as the gold's recaptured, there's only a few get their hands on it.' So they were always pestering Manlius to tell them where all this money was hidden. He put them off, saying that he would tell them soon enough. But this was the only thing they really cared about. If Manlius was telling the truth, then clearly he would receive their undying gratitude. But if he was not, he would be very far from popular.

When Aulus Cornelius Cossus left the army and arrived in Rome as Dictator, this was the tense situation that greeted him. Next day he called a meeting of the Senate and made sure that the senators would back him. Then he ordered them to accompany him to the comitium.* Here he took his official seat with the senators tightly packed round him. A messenger was sent to fetch Manlius. Immediately Manlius received the Dictator's summons, he passed the word to his supporters that the fight was on. As a result, he arrived in the comitium with a huge mob. With the senators on one side and the plebeians on the other, both with their attention riveted on their leaders, it looked like the line-up for a battle. When there was silence, the Dictator spoke:

'I know the Senate and myself do not often see eye to eye with the plebeians. I wish we did. But today's business concerns *you*, Marcus Manlius. I have a request to make of you and, for once, I think we may find that on this question we're all on the same side. It's about the Gauls' treasure. You claim that this would be enough to pay off the plebeians' debts in full: you also claim that the leaders of the Senate have embezzled it. Well, Marcus Manlius, far be it from me to stand in your way. In fact I'm right behind you – go on, free the Roman people from debt, find the men who are gloating over this public treasure and tear them away from their secret hoard! But perhaps you won't? Maybe you want to dip your fingers in the gold too? Or maybe the whole thing is a lie? In that case I shall have you arrested, and put an end to your career as a pedlar of false hopes for the masses.'

'I'm not so easily fooled', Manlius retorted. 'I know why you've been made Dictator. It's nothing to do with the Volsci – the Senate can always point at them as an enemy when it suits them. Nothing to do with the Latini or the Hernici either. They're only considering war because of Roman provocation. No, I'm the target, I and the Roman people. And now you've forgotten about this so-called war and are turning on me. The Dictator is championing the money-lenders against the plebeians. And because the plebeians support me you're trying to find some charge on which you can destroy me. Are you upset, Aulus Cornelius, and you, gentlemen of the Senate, by this crowd of men round me? You can easily disperse it. Each of you has only to commit an act of kindness, save a debtor, rescue one of your fellow citizens from prison, prevent a condemned man from being turned into a slave. Why not use all that money of yours to give others the bare necessities of life? But really you don't need to give anything away. Just agree to subtract the interest you've been paid so far from the original loan and accept the remainder as a final repayment. Then I'll have no more supporters than anyone

70

else. But I can feel you're puzzled: why should I be the only man to care about my fellow citizens? I don't know. You might as well ask why I was the only man to protect our defences on the Capitol. Then I was doing my best for you all: now I'm helping Romans one by one. As for the Gauls' treasure, it's a straightforward business, though your request makes it seem otherwise. Why question me on something you know all about? Why should we have to shake the money out of your purses? Bring it out yourselves, unless you've got something to hide. You seem so keen for us to find out how this "disappearing money trick" works – I'm afraid you'll steal our eyeballs while we're watching! No, it's not my job to find the missing treasure for you. *You* should be made to hand it over to the state.'

To which the Dictator replied, 'Enough of this quibbling! Either prove your accusations of theft against the Senate, or admit they're just a pack of dangerous lies.'

Manlius refused to speak at his enemy's command and the Dictator ordered him to be taken off to prison. As soon as the officer laid hands on him, Manlius cried out:

'O Jupiter, greatest and most holy one, Juno, queen of heaven, Minerva, and all you gods and goddesses who dwell in the fortress on the Capitol, will you allow your protector to be thus maltreated by his enemies? Shall this right arm, which drove the Gauls from your temples, be held in chains?"

No one could bear to look at him or listen to what he said. But the people of Rome were nothing if not law-abiding: if this was the law, then it must be obeyed. No one, not the tribunes of the people nor the plebeians themselves, dared to flout the Dictator's authority by so much as a look or a word. So Manlius was taken off to prison. But a large number of the plebeians, so we're told, went into mourning. The men let their hair and beards grow and a sullen crowd hung around the prison entrance.

The people's voice

On the battlefield the Dictator won a victory over the Volsci, but this made him less popular rather than more: 'His real victory's been here in Rome', they grumbled; 'This triumph of his is over Manlius, not the Volsci'; 'All it needed was Manlius paraded in front of his chariot.' Revolution was not far off. The Senate immediately made a voluntary effort to ease the situation by being generous: they set up a colony at Satricum for two thousand of the citizens, giving each of them nearly two acres of land. But this only made things worse. The plebeians thought there should have been more colonists with more land apiece, and that anyway it was a bribe to get them to desert Manlius. His supporters were now more conspicuous than ever, going around with filthy clothes and gloomy faces. The Dictator had, as usual, resigned after his triumph, and people felt free to say whatever they liked.

Among these openly expressed opinions was one that said the plebeians themselves were to blame: they were always raising their champions up to the stars and then, when it came to it, leaving them in the lurch. It had happened to Spurius Cassius when he wanted to distribute public land to the plebeians. It had happened to Spurius Maelius when he paid out his own money to help the starving poor. It was happening to Manlius who had found people overwhelmed by debt, and had been dragging them towards the light of freedom when he was betrayed to his enemies. The plebeians liked to fatten their heroes for the slaughter.

'Does an ex-consul have to be treated like this? Just because he wouldn't obey a Dictator's whim?'

'Maybe he was lying, and that was why he wouldn't reply. But even slaves don't go to prison for lying.'

'Remember that night? It was nearly the last night in Roman history: Gauls swarming up the Tarpeian Rock and Manlius, covered in sweat and blood, practically rescuing Jupiter from the enemy . . .'

'And each of us gave him half a pound of flour. Is that all we owe him?'

'He was almost a god to us then – calling him "Capitolinus" certainly brings him close to Jupiter. And now we're letting him lie chained up in prison, in pitch darkness, with permission to breathe as long as the executioner says so.'

'By himself he managed to save all of us. Are so many of us really powerless to save him?'

By now the crowd refused to move away from the prison even at night and there were threats to break down the doors. But, just as they were about to rescue Manlius, the Senate decided to release him. Not that this halted the revolution; it merely supplied it with a leader.

The final act
The beginning of the next year saw a period of peace between Rome and her neighbours. Both patricians and plebeians found

this a useful breathing space: the plebeians because they were not being called up to fight and so reckoned that, with Manlius' help, they might break the money-lenders' grip; the patricians because they could devote all their energy to solving the political problems. And so, with both sides more determined than ever, things were obviously coming to a head. Night and day, Manlius' house was the scene of discussions with the plebeians' leaders as to how the revolution should be organised. Manlius himself was not used to the sort of treatment he had just received. His pride was injured and he was an angry man. He was more confident too. After all, the Dictator had not dared to have him killed; and the very fact of his being in prison had made the Dictator anxious to resign his post. Even the Senate had had to release him in the end. These thoughts made him at the same time optimistic and bitter, and he set about rousing the plebeians to new heights of fury.

'Will you never realise exactly how strong you are? Even wild animals know that much about themselves! Just do some simple arithmetic: how many are there of you? And how many of them? All you have to do is show you're ready to fight and they're bound to give in. We must take risks together. As individuals, all we can look forward to are lives of oppression. How long is it going to take you to size me up? You can rely on me, every one of you. But you must see to it that I don't fall out of favour. I was your champion; but when my enemies snapped their fingers I was suddenly a nobody. There were men among you I had saved from imprisonment, but you all stood and watched while I was led off to prison. When you're facing outsiders, you really show your mettle – you believe you're good enough to dictate to them. Why is that? Because you're in the habit of fighting them for power. But against the patricians, although you may make a bid for freedom, you're not used to defending it. Even so, with some leadership and your own efforts you've so far got everything you've asked for, whether by violence or by luck. The time has come to aim higher. I declare myself "champion of the people"! I think my efforts on your behalf have earned me that title. Maybe, of course, you can think of a title that will give your leader more authority – more power to see that your wishes are answered . . .' Apparently this was the first hint that Rome might once again be ruled by a king. But it is not clear who his fellow conspirators were or how far their plans had got.

On the other side the Senate were anxiously discussing these revolutionary meetings being held, as it happened, in a private house right in the citadel. Rome's freedom was in serious danger. Most of the senators were for strong measures: 'We don't need somebody who merely enrages a public enemy by putting him in prison; we need somebody who'll sacrifice one man to prevent a civil war.'

In the end this was what they voted for, though wrapped up in milder language: 'The magistrates must ensure that no harm shall come to the republic, through Manlius' dangerous ideas.' The tribunes of the people realised that the end of democracy would mean the end of their power too, so they were willing to do whatever the Senate wanted. Both they and the consular tribunes got together to produce an answer to the problem. None of them could see any way of avoiding a confrontation – and, what is more, a violent and bloody one. Then two of the tribunes of the people made the following proposal:

'Why are we turning this into a battle between patricians and plebeians? It's really a quarrel between Rome and a single dangerous citizen. We don't need to attack the plebeians as well – better to use them as a weapon and let Manlius destroy himself by his own power. We propose to put him on trial. There's nothing the people hate more than the idea of having a king. We just have to persuade them that from our point of view they are not the enemy. We turn them from witnesses into judges. And as soon as they realise that we, the accusers, are plebeians, while the accused is a patrician who might want to make himself king . . . you'll find their freedom is more important to them than any feelings of personal loyalty.'

The Senate passed this resolution and Manlius was put on trial. To begin with the plebeians reacted strongly. Manlius was made to wear dirty clothes and not one of the senators, nor his own family, not even his own brothers, would visit him. The plebeians were shocked to see Manlius' closest friends not in mourning – a flagrant breach of tradition. They came to the conclusion there must be a conspiracy against Manlius because he was the first patrician ever to change sides.

The day of the trial arrived. What happened then is, I think, interesting. Because he wanted to become king, all the brave and kind things Manlius had done came to seem pointless, shameful even. Apparently he produced nearly four hundred men as witnesses to his generosity: he had lent them money interest-free, saving their property and rescuing them from slavery. As for his war decorations, there was no need to describe those. He brought them into court for everyone to see. There were some thirty sets of equipment from enemies he had killed and about forty official decorations, including ten military crowns: two for being the first over the enemy walls, eight for saving his comrades' lives. After a passionate speech he bared his battle-scarred chest and turned his eyes towards the Capitol.

'Jupiter', he prayed, 'and all you other gods, I beseech your help! In this, my time of need, inspire the Roman people with the spirit you gave me, that night I saved them on the Capitol. And you, men of Rome; cast your eyes, every one of you, on that stronghold up there – and may the gods guide you as you pass judgment upon me!'

The voting then began in the Campus Martius. Manlius had finished making speeches, but he was still praying to the gods with his arms held out towards the Capitol. The tribunes realised that while the man's bravery was, so to speak, right before their eyes, there was no hope of their finding him guilty, however much he deserved it. So the vote was postponed. When they did meet again, it was in a wood outside one of the city gates. It was impossible to see the Capitol from there. This time the facts spoke for themselves. Reluctantly, sadly, bitterly, they condemned him. He was convicted, some say, as a traitor to his country. The tribunes took him and flung him down from the Tarpeian Rock – a monument to his finest hour and to his final punishment.

> We saw earlier how Coriolanus was faced with a choice between his family and his adopted country. Livy was obviously fond of such stories. As he saw it, a Roman had a strong duty to Rome. Perhaps he saw patriotism as the only cure for civil wars like the one he had lived through as a young man.
>
> The next story is dated around 336. Across the Adriatic Sea, Alexander the Great was taking over after the death of his father and preparing to conquer the world. In Italy, Rome was moving more slowly towards an empire, with a large number of wars against her neighbours, including the tribes of Latium (the Latini) to the south (see map, p. 6). Titus Manlius belonged to the same family as Marcus Manlius Capitolinus, but was probably two or three generations younger.

LOVE AND DUTY

An insult repaid

Both Senate and people now agreed to declare war on the Latins. The consuls enlisted two armies and camped near Capua, where the Latins and their allies were massing their troops.

The senior Roman officers were insistent that in this campaign, out of all the ones the Romans had fought in their history, it was absolutely vital for the men to obey orders. Their anxiety was increased by the fact that they were facing Latins, whose language, upbringing, weapons and armour, and above all military organisation, were the same as their own. Soldier had served with soldier, centurion with centurion, tribune with tribune as equals and comrades in the same garrison and often in the same section. In case this similarity led the Romans to mistake friends for enemies or *vice versa*, the consuls made an official announcement that there were to be no private raids.

Company commanders were sent out to make a thorough inspection of the surrounding country. One of them was Titus Manlius, the consul's son. He led his cavalry almost to within a spear's throw of the nearest enemy outpost. This was occupied by cavalry from Tusculum under the command of Geminus Maecius. His reputation among his men was considerable, since he was a nobleman and had a fine war record. Now, all the leading officers on both sides knew each other, so when he spotted the Roman cavalry he also recognised the consul's son at their head.

'Are you going to take on the lot of us with that handful? You might leave something for the consuls and their two armies!'

'They'll be here when they're needed', replied Titus, 'and I promise you, when our two armies do meet, you won't find it so amusing.'

Geminus then rode out a few paces in front of his men and said: 'While we're waiting for the great day when you actually get your armies moving, why don't we two have a private fight? Between us we can demonstrate how much tougher Latin cavalry is than Roman.'

Titus reacted instantly. Whether it was anger, or shame at refusing such a challenge, or Fate, no man can say. Forgetting his father's orders, indeed the official announcement of both consuls, he hurled himself into the attack; although in fact it was not going to make much difference to him whether he won or lost. The troops stood well back as though they were watching a show. Across the space between them, lances poised, the two leaders spurred their horses on to the fight. At the first charge Titus' lance scraped his enemy's helmet and Geminus' grazed the neck of Titus' horse. Then, on the turn for the second charge, Titus was the quicker to attack and drove his lance at the horse's forehead. The animal reared up on its hind legs. With a great toss of its head it threw Geminus crashing to the ground. He struggled to get to his feet, heaving himself up with the help of lance and shield. But Titus struck at his throat with such fury that the lance came out through his ribcage and pinned him to the ground. Titus then stripped the corpse and rejoined his men.

Father and son

Surrounded by a cheering mob, he returned to camp and reported back to his father at headquarters, not knowing what the future held for him: praise or punishment?

'Father', he said, 'I was challenged to mounted combat and I have killed and stripped my enemy. Here I bring you his armour and weapons, for all to see that I am a true son of yours.'

At once the consul dismissed his son and ordered the trumpet to sound the 'fall in'. When the whole camp was on parade, he spoke:

'Titus Manlius, you have shown lack of respect both for the command of the consuls and for my authority as your father. You were ordered to refrain from private hostilities with the enemy. You have done your best to destroy the military discipline on which the strength of Rome has always depended. You leave me with two alternatives: I must ignore either the needs of Rome or my feelings for you. I cannot allow the safety of the state to be undermined just to keep my conscience clear – if I must suffer for this crime, then I must. It will be a bitter lesson for other young men, but a necessary one. Believe me, I love you and admire your bravery, even though it has led you to pursue an empty vision of glory. Nevertheless the choice is clear. If you die, the consuls' authority will be confirmed. If you are pardoned, it will be gone for ever. If there is a drop of my blood in your veins, I cannot imagine that you will refuse to help restore the military discipline which your own disobedience has endangered – lictor, tie him to the stake!'

The whole parade was stunned at this appalling command. The soldiers were hushed not by discipline but by fear; aghast, silent, motionless, as though each man felt the axe poised above his own head. But suddenly, as the blood spurted from the severed neck, a furious, continuous roar went up of wailing and cursing. They dressed the young man's body in the armour he had won, built a funeral pyre outside the camp and cremated him with all military honours. The 'orders of Manlius' not only struck terror into those who were there. They provided a fearful warning for future generations.

Even so, this brutal punishment tightened up the soldiers' obedience to their general. The whole organisation of guards and look-outs became stricter and even the Romans' discipline in the final battle was improved by the consul's savage example. Once the war had been brought to a successful end, with rewards and punishments duly distributed, Manlius returned to Rome. They say he was met by a deputation consisting entirely of older men. Then and for the rest of his life the young men shunned him and spoke of him with curses.

5 The conquest of the Samnites

Livy's *History* is full of battles. Some of them are dull, and some very hard to follow. Our last extract is reasonably straightforward and it also shows the kind of story Livy was particularly good at telling: a story where what happens depends largely on the people involved, on their characters and their emotions. 'War, like peace, has its rules', declared Camillus in an earlier story. 'The Caudine Forks' suggests that when war gets mixed up with politics, the rules are not so easy to make.

THE CAUDINE FORKS: c. 321 B.C.

The trap

And so we come to an important year in Rome's history: one that saw first a military disaster and then the Treaty of Caudium. The consuls were Titus Veturius Calvinus and Spurius Postumius. On the Samnites' side, the general was Gaius Pontius. He was the toughest fighter and the best leader they had while his father, Herennius, was their shrewdest tactician. The Samnites had sent negotiators over to the Romans to try and arrange a peace treaty. They failed to do so. On their return, Pontius made the following speech:

'You mustn't regard this mission as a failure. If the gods were angry because we broke the previous treaty, we have now brought them back on to our side. Men of Samnium, we have no choice but war. And since we *must* fight, we are *right* to fight. The gods' approval is an important factor in everything a man does. It could be that so far you have been fighting more against the gods than against men. But now . . . I can promise you, in the war that lies ahead, the gods themselves shall be your leaders!'

With these encouraging words (true enough, as it turned out) he set off at the head of his army. They camped, in the utmost secrecy, in the area round Caudium. He'd heard that the Roman consuls and their troops were encamped near Calatia. So he sent ten soldiers off in that direction dressed up as shepherds. Each

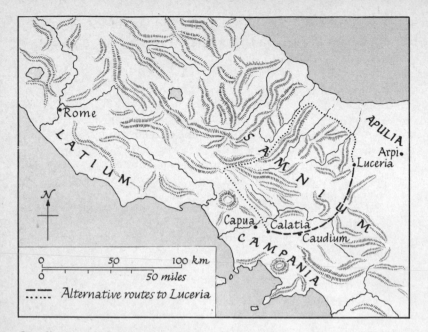

Caudium and the surrounding area

had a flock of sheep with him and the orders were to split up and then graze the sheep within reach of the Roman camp. Whenever Roman soldiers left camp to find food, the 'shepherds' were all to tell the same story: the Samnite army was down in Apulia; they were blockading Luceria with every available man, and the place was about to surrender. This rumour had been circulating for some time. What the shepherds said, and the fact that they *all* said it, made the Romans think the rumour must be true. Obviously they had to help the people of Luceria, who were reliable allies. At the same time they had to stop the whole of Apulia being overrun. The only question was: which route should they take?

There were two possible roads to Luceria. One followed the line of the Adriatic coast. It was a straightforward march through flat country, safe but on the long side. The other, shorter way was through the Caudine Forks. These consist of two deep, narrow ravines, covered in trees and hemmed in on both sides by mountains. Between the ravines lies a fairly large, grassy plain with streams running through it. The road runs across the middle of this plain, but to get to it you first have to negotiate one of the ravines. Then you have either to go back the way you came, or (assuming you have entered the western end of the plain) to march through the ravine at the eastern end, which is narrower and even harder going.

The Romans headed for the plain, struggling along the western ravine and marching straight on to the one at the other end. A mass of fallen trees and huge boulders barred their way. The Samnites' trick had worked. The Romans could actually see some of the enemy guarding the far end of the ravine. Immediately they headed back for the western entrance. There too was a manned barricade. They halted, without waiting for orders. A strange kind of paralysis came over their minds and bodies. For some time they stood there in silence, looking at each other, all waiting for someone else to make a decision.

Then the consuls' tents could be seen going up. Men got out their spades and stakes. Obviously it was ridiculous to dig themselves in – they were done for, without question – and they realised this. But it might just be a help. So they began to dig, every man for himself, with no encouragement or orders from anyone. A camp duly materialised by one of the streams, while the enemy shouted rude remarks. Even the Romans could not resist making sour jokes at their own useless labour. The consuls were desperate. They did not even call a meeting, as there was nothing to discuss and nothing to hope for. But the officers and military tribunes had a meeting of their own, while the soldiers demanded that their leaders 'do something'; a demand which even the immortal gods would have had a job to satisfy.

Night fell and still there was no move towards a solution, only moans and private mutterings:

'Why don't we attack the barricades? We could get up these mountains with our weapons, through the trees. Just let's get to grips with these Samnites – we've been beating them for nearly thirty years! Everything will sort itself out once we can fight those vermin face to face.'

'There's no way out and nowhere to go. Unless of course you can just shove the mountains out of the way! But as long as these cliffs are towering over us, how are you going to get to grips? Weapons, courage – what's the point? We're all prisoners and we're all beaten. The Samnites aren't even going to fight. At least then we could die honourably. No, all they have to do is sit and wait.'

This sort of talk went on all night. No one felt like eating or sleeping.

Herennius

The Samnites, too, were nonplussed by their success. So they all agreed to send a message to Herennius, Pontius' father, and ask his advice. Herennius was a very old man. His years as soldier and statesman were behind him and his body was showing the signs of age. His mind, however, was as sharp as ever. Pontius' messenger delivered the news:

'The Roman armies have been hemmed in between the two ravines in the Caudine Forks. What should we do now?'

Herennius replied: 'Let them all go immediately, unharmed.'

The Samnites refused to do this, so the messenger came back and asked again.

'Kill the lot!' said the old man.

This was the kind of riddle you get when you go and consult an oracle. Pontius assumed that old age had moved beyond his father's body and finally reached his brain. But everyone else wanted Herennius to come and advise them in person, so Pontius gave in. Herennius made no objection and, so we are told, was brought to the Samnite camp in a cart. He joined in the council of war and made a forthright speech. His advice was the same; now he merely added the reasons behind it:

'If you follow my first proposal – which is what I recommend – then you will be doing a great favour to a very powerful nation. This will ensure lasting peace and friendship between us. If you decide on my second proposal, you will be postponing the war for several generations. Even then Rome won't easily replace the manpower of two armies. There's no third course of action open to you.'

But Pontius and the other leaders pressed him for his advice on a third course: namely, letting the Romans go unharmed but making them pay some kind of penalty for their defeat.

'That way', said Herennius, 'you won't win friends or get rid of enemies. Suppose you insult them and let them go – then what? The Roman people are not the sort to take failure quietly. Whatever you force them to do in their present desperate situation, they won't forget. Their pride won't let them rest until you've paid for your action many times over.'

The Samnites ignored both of his proposals and Herennius was taken back home.

Meanwhile the Romans had made a number of futile attempts to escape. They were beginning to suffer from a general shortage of supplies, so they had no choice but to send negotiators to try and arrange a fair settlement. If the Samnites refused to consider peace, then they must be provoked into fighting. To which Pontius replied:

'There is no war. It's over. You've lost, you're prisoners, and *still* you can't face facts! Very well, I shall make each of you go under the yoke, unarmed and with just one piece of clothing. Otherwise, the terms will be the same for both sides. You take yourselves and your colonies out of Samnium, and then each of us can live peacefully side by side under our own laws. These are my terms. If you agree, I'll make a treaty with your consuls. But if there's anything here you can't accept, don't waste your time coming to see me again!'

A terrible groan went up from the Roman army when they heard the news. They were plunged into the depths of misery. The scene could not have been more melancholy if they had all been facing execution on the spot.

The consuls then went to negotiate with Pontius. He wanted to have a signed treaty. But the consuls explained there could be no treaty without the Roman people's permission. Even after that, priests would have to sanctify the treaty with the usual ceremonies. Therefore some delay was bound to occur. So the Samnites insisted on taking hostages – six hundred cavalrymen – and it was understood that if the Romans broke their word, these six hundred would be killed. A date was fixed for the handover, and for the procession under the yoke.

The day of shame

The consuls' return to camp was the signal for further demonstrations of grief, and very nearly of violence.

'But for the consuls' stupidity we shouldn't be here.'

'The cowards . . . thanks to them, we're in like a lion and out like a lamb!'

'No guides, no reconnaissance. It was like wild animals being driven into a trap.'

'Look at us! With no weapons, helpless, at the enemy's mercy . . . I can just hear the Samnites laughing at us as we go under the yoke, and see the sneers on their faces.'

'And after we've escaped their swords, then we'll have to crawl for help to some friendly city or other. Not to mention going back to Rome and our families – when you think how many times we've returned in triumph, and our ancestors . . .'

'Giving up without a wound or a battle, it's unheard of.

Equipment, strength, courage, all utterly wasted!'

They were still complaining bitterly when the dreadful moment arrived. It was to be even worse than they had feared. To begin with, they were ordered to strip down to their tunics, leave their swords behind, and assemble outside the ditch surrounding the camp. The six hundred hostages were handed over and taken away under guard. Then, the lictors were told to leave their consuls' side, and the two commanding officers were stripped of their general's cloaks. A few minutes before, their men had been cursing them, saying they ought to be turned over to the Samnites and tortured. But as their cloaks were removed, the men's mood softened. Each one for the moment forgot his own troubles. Each one turned his eyes away. For the greatest office in Rome to be insulted like this! Even to look seemed like a crime.

The consuls, more or less half-naked, went under the yoke first; then their junior officers in order of rank; finally, the legionaries one by one. The Samnites stood around, fully armed, swearing and poking fun at their victims. Many of the Romans had swords waved in their faces. Some were wounded, some even killed, for allowing their emotions to show too plainly on their faces.

So the deed was done and, what was almost the worst part, the Samnites saw it all. When the Romans did emerge from the western ravine, they looked like men who had escaped from the underworld, seeing sunlight for the first time. But by this same light they could see the appalling spectacle of their comrades. Death, in whatever form, was a brighter prospect.

The Roman army could easily have reached Capua before dark. However, they were not sure what sort of reception they would get. Shame, too, held them back. Instead, they threw themselves down by the road just outside the town, with no supplies of any kind. The people round Capua were not known for their natural sympathy. But the Romans were their allies, and pity got the better of them. Immediately they brought proper uniforms for the consuls and generous supplies of weapons, horses, clothes and food for the men. As the Romans approached Capua, the whole government and people came out to meet them. It was a kind and friendly reception at every level. But this show of goodwill, smiling faces, and gentle words had no effect. The Romans would not speak. They would not even look up and meet the eyes of those who were trying to comfort them. It was more than grief. It was a kind of shame that made crowds and conversation unbearable.

84

Homecoming

Next day some of the young Capuan noblemen accompanied the Romans to the border of their territory. When the escort got back to Capua, they delivered a report to the leaders of the government:

'Our impression was that they were much gloomier and more dejected than yesterday. They marched in silence, like mutes. That famous Roman courage has vanished – left behind with their weapons, maybe. We greeted them and questioned them, but couldn't get any answer. Their shame wouldn't even let them mutter. You'd have thought each of them was carrying that yoke round his neck! This Samnite victory is more than remarkable, it's permanent. The Gauls, as we know, captured Rome. The Samnites have done far more than that: they've captured her courage and her fighting spirit.'

By now the terrible news had reached Rome. The first report had said the Romans were surrounded. At once, the city began to call up more troops. Then came worse news – worse, that is, not because of any danger, but because of the disgraceful terms on which peace had been obtained. At this point the call-up was abandoned. Immediately, and spontaneously, the city went into mourning. The shops round the forum were shut and all business suspended, before anyone could announce it officially. Senators and knights removed their badges of office. As for the citizens, they felt the disgrace almost more deeply than the army did. They were angry with the generals and those who had organised the surrender. More than that, they were furious with the common soldiers, who were in no way to blame; there was talk of not letting them back into Rome or their own houses.

Then the soldiers returned. They were a miserable sight, enough to soften the angriest heart. They gave no sign of relief at being safely back home. Their appearance and expression were those of prisoners. Reaching Rome late in the evening, they slunk off to their homes. The next day and for several days afterwards none of them showed himself in the forum or in the streets. The consuls too retired from public life, but the Senate insisted they must appoint a Dictator to organise the election for two new consuls. Eventually these were elected: Quintus Publilius Philo (for the third time) and Lucius Papirius Cursor (for the second time) – both popular choices, as they were among the most outstanding politicians of their age.

The Senate demanded that these two should take control of the situation right from the day they were elected. Once the usual ceremonies were over, they turned to the business of Caudium. Publilius was the chairman and called first on Spurius Postumius, one of the ex-consuls. Postumius rose to his feet. His face held the same expression as it had going under the yoke.

'I know', he said, 'only too well why you, the consuls, have asked me to open this debate. It's a sign of disgrace, not honour. And I stand here not as a senator, but as a man guilty of two crimes: an unsuccessful war, and a shameful peace. Not that I should have any trouble explaining what has happened – after all, you've had some experience yourselves of the part Fate plays in men's lives. But in fact our crime and punishment are not on the agenda. So I needn't start a plea for the defence. Instead, I'd like to make a brief proposal. Did I surrender just to save my own skin, or the lives of your soldiers? Was this agreement shocking, or unavoidable? My proposal should help you decide. The point is that the surrender took place without the Roman people's approval. So, they are not bound by its terms. All the Samnites are entitled to are the bodies of my colleague and myself. I propose, therefore, that the Roman war priests* should strip us, tie our hands together and deliver us to the enemy. Then Rome will not be bound by any religious duty; and nothing, in heaven or on earth, will prevent you from continuing this just and righteous war.'

REVIVAL

Postumius' suggestion, helped by his gift for words, had its effect on the Senate. The tribunes of the people too were persuaded to put their lives at the senators' disposal and resigned their posts straight away. The war priests then took charge of them, until their return to Caudium. As soon, as the Senate had taken this step, it was as if a bright light began to shine down on Rome. Everywhere people were talking about Postumius. He was the hero of the hour. His initiative and his example had saved the city from a shameful peace; to save Rome, he was offering himself as the Samnites' victim, for whatever tortures their fury might invent. War was in every Roman's heart, and nothing but war. How long before they could fight the Samnites face to face?

In this angry mood, an army was collected almost entirely of volunteers. The same soldiers were now spread in different groups through the legions. Led by the war priests, they marched to Caudium. They came to the camp gate and the priests gave their orders:

'Those responsible for the peace will now be stripped, and their hands tied behind them!'

The officer in charge of Postumius, remembering he was dealing with an ex-consul, tied his hands loosely.

'Tighter than that!' shouted Postumius. 'This must be a real surrender.'

The procession then made its way to the Samnite assembly, where Pontius was presiding. One of the war priests, Aulus Cornelius Arvina, explained why the Romans had come:

'These men have guaranteed a treaty, without the Roman people's permission. In doing so, they have committed a crime. The Roman people must be cleared of all guilt arising from this crime. I therefore deliver these men into your hands.'

As he finished his speech, Postumius brought up his knee and gave the priest a fierce kick on the upper part of his leg.

'I am a Samnite citizen', Postumius declared loudly, 'and by kicking that Roman official I have broken international law. Now the Romans can fight with a clear conscience.'

'I refuse to accept this surrender', replied Pontius, 'and so will my people. And you, Postumius, if you really believe there *are* gods, must either reject the whole agreement or stick to it. All those Roman prisoners are, by rights, still the property of Samnium. Otherwise the agreement stands. Not that I should be making these points to you – you show the greatest honesty in surrendering yourself to us. No, I address myself to the Roman people. If they now regret the promises made at the Forks, then they should put the legions back into the ravine where they were surrounded. That would be perfectly fair. We can start all over again. The Romans can have the weapons they handed over, they can go back inside their camp, they can have everything they had the day before the discussions started. *Then* they can start talking about war and rejecting the peace formula! We're happy to fight from this initial position. The Roman people needn't blame the consuls and their agreement, we needn't doubt the honour of the Roman people.

Are you always going to find reasons, every time you're beaten, why you shouldn't keep your word? You gave Porsenna hostages, and got them back by trickery. You used gold to buy Rome back from the Gauls, and while they had it in their hands you slaughtered them. You promised us peace, providing we returned your legions to you. Now you say this peace is cancelled. And all your tricks have that bit of legal dressing on top!

Very well, go to war because Postumius has just dug his knee into a Roman official! And the gods will all think Postumius is a Samnite, not a Roman, and that a Roman official has been insulted by a Samnite, and so you are right to attack us! This is turning religion upside down. You, as old men and ex-consuls, should be ashamed of spouting such childish riddles, just to get out of your promises. Untie these Romans! They can go whenever they want.'

So the group of Romans were, as far as their own promises went, now free. Whether they were free in their capacity as citizens of Rome is another matter. But anyway they left Caudium and reached the Roman camp without trouble.

The Samnites realised then what had happened. They had exchanged a peace in which they were the masters for renewed war of the bitterest kind. They could see the future course of the war practically laid out before them. Well might they wish they had taken Herennius' good advice! But it was too late now. By steering between his two proposals, they had sacrificed actual victory for an unstable peace. There had been no fighting since the surrender at Caudium, and both sides had equal chances. But morale had shifted. With a bloodless victory to Pontius' credit, his reputation in Samnium was still outshone by Postumius' in Rome, surrender or no. For the Romans, the very fact they could fight again was as good as a promise of victory; and by the same token the Samnites saw Rome's revival as an omen of the worst.

A STRAIGHT FIGHT

The Roman consuls took charge of one area each. Papirius marched to Apulia, heading for Luceria, where the six hundred Roman hostages were being held. Publilius stayed in Samnium to deal with the enemy in the area of the Forks. This put the Samnites in a quandary. If they went east to Luceria, the Romans might attack them from behind. But if they did not, Luceria might be taken. In the end they decided on a straight fight with Publilius, so they took up their battle positions.

Publilius was ready to face them. But first he thought he ought to assemble his army for some encouraging remarks. The Romans came running – only you could not hear a word of the consul's speech for shouts of 'Let's get on with the fight!' Memory of their disgrace was encouragement enough for all of them. So they turned towards the enemy. The standard-bearers were pushed on from behind, and there was to be no waiting while javelins were thrown or swords unsheathed. As one man they threw their javelins away and raced towards the Samnites, swords at the ready. Publilius had no chance to work out tactics or post reserves. The Romans were like madmen, sweeping everything before them in their fury. The Samnites turned and ran. They did not even stop at their camp, but scattered in the direction of Apulia. Then they collected themselves and reached Luceria together. The Romans' headlong rush took them through the Samnite army and right into their camp. Here they dealt out more bloodshed and slaughter than they had on the battlefield, and destroyed most of the valuables they found in their rage.

The other Roman army was under the command of Papirius. They marched down the coast as far as Arpi and found everything quiet. This was not because the Romans had done the population any favours, more that the Samnites' cruelty had made them hated. Papirius duly reached Luceria, followed by his colleague. The arrival of this second army brought the Samnites serious problems over supplies. It meant that while Papirius kept the blockade going, the other consul was free to roam the countryside and stop food getting through. The Samnites in their camp outside Luceria grew desperate: if the blockade continued, they would have to give in or starve. So they massed their forces and prepared to fight.

The consuls divided the Roman troops between them and began an all-out attack on the Samnite camp. They tore out the stakes from the earth-wall and began to throw earth and stakes into the ditch beyond. This was more than native courage – disgrace had set a fury gnawing at their hearts. Then they were in, and it was every man for himself. No Forks here, no Caudium, no fatal traps for the unwary! They knew it was purely a matter of Roman bravery, and it took more than walls and ditches to stop that. Whether the Samnites fought or ran, whether armed or not, slaves, ex-slaves, adults, children, men, animals – all fell to the Roman sword. No living thing would have survived if the consuls had not sounded the retreat. The soldiers were thirsting for blood and orders had to be reinforced with threats to get them out of the camp. Revenge was sweet and they were furious at being interrupted. The consuls realised a swift explanation was called for:

'None of you hates the Samnites, or ever will hate them, more than we do. We have led you in war, and we would lead you on to vengeance without end. *But* . . . we must not forget the six hundred Roman hostages still held in Luceria. Once the Samnites see we're going to show no mercy, then in desperation they may kill before they can be killed.'

At this there were shouts of agreement, and relief that their bloodlust had been checked. Anything was better than losing so many of Rome's finest warriors.

The soldiers were dismissed and the officers held a council of war. Should they use every available man to keep the blockade tight? Or should one of the consuls go round the Apulian tribes with his army and find out whose side they were on? They decided on this second plan. So Publilius marched through Apulia and in this one expedition settled matters with a number of tribes, whether by force or friendly agreement. Papirius in the meantime went on with the blockade. Here things turned out exactly as he had hoped. He managed to block all the supply routes from Samnium and the garrison in Luceria was on the point of starvation. A deputation came to Papirius: they would release the hostages (which was what the fight was about) if he would lift the blockade.

'Really', Papirius replied, 'you should have gone to Pontius, son of Herennius – the man who sent the Romans under the yoke. He's the expert at deciding how losers should be punished! But as you've come to me instead and want to know what I think is fair, well, you can take this message back to Luceria: I want weapons, equipment, pack animals and all civilians left inside the town; then I intend to have the soldiers stripped to their tunics and sent under the yoke. As you know, there's nothing new about this. We're just paying back a debt.'

The Samnites could not refuse. Seven thousand of them went under the yoke. In Luceria the Romans found huge quantities of valuables, as well as all the standards and weapons they had lost at Caudium. Best of all, they found the six hundred hostages unharmed.

Altogether, in the way the Romans snatched victory from the jaws of defeat, this story is one of the most amazing in all their history. And some of the versions I have found add a finishing touch – which may be true. According to them Pontius, son of

Herennius, general of the Samnites, gave the Roman consuls compensation for their disgrace. He, too, was sent under the yoke.

After this victory Rome soon became mistress of central Italy. Though the Samnites did challenge her again they were never a serious threat. More dangerous was a mercenary army hired by the Greek town of Tarentum in southern Italy. It was led by King Pyrrhus of Greece who was the first person to employ elephants against the Roman army. But he too had to give way to Roman courage, which next had to face the Carthaginians in Sicily. But that is another story.

Glossary

as: Originally a bronze coin, weighing one pound (½ kg), but gradually reduced in size and value. There were at first ten *asses* to a *denarius*, the silver coin of Rome, and later eighteen.

Campus Martius: Originally pasture land outside the city boundary, in a bend of the Tiber. It was a flat open plain, where the Roman army mustered.

Capitol: One of the hills of Rome, which served both as a defensive citadel and as a religious centre: on it was the great temple dedicated to Jupiter Optimus Maximus, Juno and Minerva.

centurion: The senior non-commissioned officer of the Roman army, nominally in command of a century (which numbered sixty to eighty men in Caesar's army).

city prefect: A temporary deputy of the king or consuls when they were absent from Rome.

comitium: A place adjacent to the forum, where the people voted.

consul: One of the two senior magistrates of the Roman state: they were elected annually after the expulsion of the kings.

Dictator: A magistrate elected in times of emergency, holding office for a maximum of six months. They had absolute authority, superior to that of any other magistrate.

duumvir: One of any committee or court consisting of two members.

forum: The public meeting-place, or market, in the centre of Rome.

Games: *Ludi*: festivities, usually with a religious origin, in which formal physical activities – athletics, dancing, drama or gladiatorial combats – were held in honour of a god.

lictor: An attendant of a magistrate, granted as a sign of official dignity. Each of the consuls was attended by twelve lictors, carrying a bundle of rods (*fasces*) from which an axe projected. Apart from walking in front of the consuls, their task was to carry out judicial sentences, e.g. scourging, beheading.

military tribune: The senior officers of the legion, elected by the people: there were six to a legion.

Neptune: The Italian god of water, identified with Poseidon, the Greek god of earthquakes and water, who was also sometimes honoured as god of horses.

oracle: The answer given by any god to those who consulted him. Also the place at which these answers were given; for example, the shrine of the Pythia, in or near the temple of Apollo at Delphi in central Greece.

patricians: Members of a privileged class at Rome: the name probably derives from the use of *pater* ('father') to mean 'member of the Senate'.

Quirinus: Probably the god of the settlement that preceded the foundation of Rome: he ranked third after Jupiter and Mars.

Senate: The council of senior citizens and ex-magistrates, which took over supreme power in Rome after the expulsion of the kings. It was formerly restricted to the patricians, but plebeians were admitted quite frequently in the fourth century B.C. Traditionally it began with one hundred members, but the number soon increased to three hundred. Its members were forbidden to take part in trade.

soothsayer: An official supposedly able to foretell the future from the inspection of animals offered in sacrifice.

standard: A pole, topped with various emblems or banners, carried in front of every military unit, whether maniple, cohort or legion. To carry it was an honour; the standard-bearer was thus a man of some consequence.

tribune of the people: There were originally two but soon ten. They were elected to defend the lives and property of the people. Their power came from the oath sworn by the plebeians to protect the lives of the tribunes. They had the right of *veto*, that is, they could forbid the act of any magistrate except the Dictator.

Vesta: Goddess of the hearth. Her temple at Rome (the hearth of the state) was round, containing no statue, but only a fire, which supposedly was never allowed to go out. She was served by six Vestal Virgins, who were appointed for thirty years, during which time they had to remain virgin.

war priests: The *Fetiales*, a priesthood responsible for the ritual proclamation of war and confirming of peace treaties.

yoke: Two upright spears, stuck in the ground, with a third tied across the top. A vanquished army was made to pass beneath the yoke as a symbol of humiliation.

DATE DUE

DATE DUE		
DEC 1 4 1983		
FEB 1 5 1984		
JUN 2 8 1989		
APR 2 4 1961		
AUG 2 1 1992		
DEC 0 9 2005		